The Reward Management Toolkit

A step-by-step guide to designing and delivering pay and benefits

Michael Armstrong
and Ann Cummins

KoganPage

LONDON PHILADELPHIA NEW DELHI

D0071334

First published in Great Britain and the United States in 2011 by Kogan Page Limited

120 Pentonville Road
London N1 9JN
United Kingdom
www.koganpage.com

525 South 4th Street, #241
Philadelphia PA 19147
USA

4737/23 Ansari Road
Daryaganj
New Delhi 110002
India

ISBN   978 0 7494 6167 6
E-ISBN 978 0 7494 6168 3

British Library Cataloguing-in-Publication Data

A CIP record for this book is available from the British Library.

Library of Congress Cataloging-in-Publication Data

Armstrong, Michael, 1928–
    The reward management toolkit : a step-by-step guide to designing and delivering pay and benefits / Michael Armstrong, Ann Cummins.
        p. cm.
    ISBN 978-0-7494-6167-6 -- ISBN 978-0-7494-6168-3 (ebook)   1. Compensation management. 2. Incentives in industry.   3. Employee motivation.   I. Cummins, Ann, 1959–   II. Title.
    HF5549.5.C67A7614 2010
    658.3′2–dc22

                                                                                        2010033367

Typeset by Graphicraft Limited, Hong Kong

CONTENTS

Tool 08   Contingent pay 133

Tool 09   Bonus schemes 151

Tool 10   Executive remuneration 173

LIST OF FIGURES

To access the templates used in this book go to
www.koganpage.com/TheRewardManagementToolkit
and use the password TRMT002

Introduction: the tools and how they are used

The purpose of this book of reward tools is to provide practical guidance on the steps required to develop and implement reward innovations and to manage key reward practices. In each of the main areas of reward management, tools are provided in the form of questionnaires and checklists that can be used to conduct reward surveys, to analyse reward arrangements and the context in which they take place, to assist in the diagnosis of problems and issues, to plan development and implementation programmes, to assess risks, and to evaluate reward effectiveness.

These instruments can be used by internal HR or reward specialists or external consultants involved in developing or evaluating reward systems. Importantly, they can play an essential part in the involvement of people in these processes through attitude surveys, focus groups, workshops and project teams.

This introduction includes:

- a map of the overall structure of the tools;
- a description of the structure of individual tools;
- a review of the basic considerations affecting the use of the tools;
- suggestions on how the tools can be used;
- guidelines on the use of the tools in consultative/involvement processes.

Overall structure of the tools

The overall structure of the tools is shown in Figure 0.1.

FIGURE 0.1 Overall structure of tools

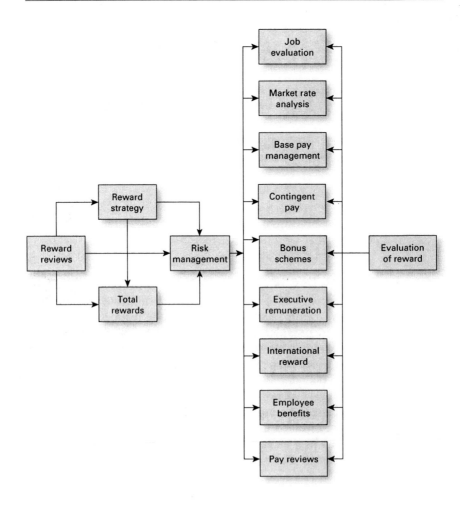

Individual structure of tools

Each tool is divided into the following sections:

- Introduction: a definition of the subject area covered by the tool.
- The purpose and contents of the tool.
- The sequence of steps or activities required to achieve the purpose of the tool. This includes surveys, questionnaires and checklists.

Basic considerations in using the tools

The two significant considerations affecting the use of the tools are involvement and communication.

Involvement

People support what they help to create. This is the argument for involving employees in the review and development of reward practices and is an underlying theme in the tools. It means giving employees a voice in matters that affect them. These include reward practices, which fundamentally shape the employment relationship.

As the work of Purcell *et al* (2003) demonstrates, the key factor in high-performance organizations is how they use reward and other HR practices to support a positive workplace climate in which employees voluntarily commit to deliver those levels of performance. It's no use having a well-designed incentive plan in a workplace if employees don't feel involved and are never consulted on how the performance the plan measures might be improved. They, not the incentive plan – nor even, dare one say, their managers – produce those improvements.

Involvement in reward management can be achieved through joint consultation, surveys, focus groups, workshops and project teams or task forces as described in the final section of this introduction.

Communication

Another recurrent theme in the tools is the need for good communication. Armstrong and Brown (2006) produced three reasons why this is significant:

- Reward can be a technically complex field, and moves towards total rewards and the greater tailoring and personalization of reward packages make full employee understanding both more important but also more difficult to achieve.
- If staff do not understand their rewards arrangements, then employers are not investing what is generally their largest cost item in an effective way.
- Rewards are an emotive issue. So many personal needs are tied up in them – security, recognition, status and so on – that discussion of and particularly changes to them almost inevitably generate emotional and sometimes hostile responses from at least some employees.

Using the tool

The tools set out a step-by-step process of analysis and diagnosis. Questionnaires and checklists are provided to elicit views, summarize arrangements and issues and provide a framework for decision making. However, the process of reviewing and developing rewards is in practice not always as sequential as the layouts of the tools suggest. The tools should not, indeed cannot, be used rigidly. It is often a case of using the tool flexibly in accordance with the circumstances.

It is useful in the first place to read through the whole tool to understand its structure and gain familiarity with the instruments it contains. How it is used can then be planned in accordance with the requirements presented by the situation facing the organization. They need to take account of priorities imposed by internal and external pressures. A speedy solution may be required to a pressing problem and this will mean selecting the relevant parts of the tools and focusing on these. Only a limited number of the instruments may therefore be used.

The tools have been designed to provide a wide choice of instruments from which a selection can be made. These instruments contain statements or questions that are likely to be generally relevant. But these are only intended to provide guidelines and can be amended to suit the requirements of the situation. Thus questions could be added or deleted or the instrument could be shortened to ease administration.

Used on this selective basis, the tools can provide the basis for programme planning, whether it is a survey, a risk assessment exercise, a fundamental strategic review, a study of particular aspects of reward management or the evaluation of reward effectiveness. Instruments from within the tools can be selected for use in surveys and in involvement activities as described later in this introduction. They can elicit the information upon which communication plans can be based.

Use of the tools in consultative/involvement processes

The tools, especially the instruments contained within them, can play an important part in the consultative/involvement processes of joint consultation, obtaining the views of employees (attitude surveys), focus groups, workshops and project teams.

Joint consultation

Joint consultation enables managers and employee representatives to meet on a regular basis in order to exchange views, to make good use of members' knowledge and expertise, and to deal with matters of common interest. The tools can be used to identify issues of joint concern and by joint consultation committees as a framework for discussion.

Meaningful consultation involves the following actions by management:

- Inform employees of what management is thinking of doing (not intending to do).
- Get employees involved in analysing and discussing the issues (with the help of the tools).
- Give employees sufficient time to respond.
- Give consideration to the employees' response.
- Explain fully the response of management to the employees' view.

Attitude surveys

An attitude survey is a valuable method of obtaining the views of employees about the reward system. It is important to ensure that:

- the key items to be covered are identified and defined;
- the questions are clearly worded and unequivocal;
- there are not too many questions – lengthy and over-elaborate surveys reduce response levels;
- undue repetition is avoided although it can be useful to seek a supplementary view to reinforce the response to a key question (this may involve changing a positive question into a negative one or vice versa);
- responses can be readily analysed – a Likert scale is recommended (which records the views of respondents on the extent to which they agree or disagree with a statement); many surveys use a five-point scale but some compilers prefer a four-point scale to avoid the tendency to centralize responses;
- avoid relying on qualitative questions (ie those asking for a written view rather than ticking a Likert scale box) – such questions can provide useful information about opinions but they are more difficult to analyse and can put off respondents;
- explain carefully the reasons for the survey and how it will be used – emphasize that it will be anonymous;
- without prejudicing anonymity in any way, obtain some information about the function in which employees work and their level, eg manager, supervisor, as a basis for more detailed analysis;
- feed back summaries of the results, including negative views, to all employees (or at least to those who participated);
- use the outcome of the survey as the basis for discussions with employees in focus groups or workshops;

- inform employees of any actions taken as a result of the survey and subsequent discussions.

Focus groups

Focus groups generate discussion amongst a small number of people (typically six to eight) on key questions. They can go more deeply into issues and enable a more comprehensive analysis to take place of the differing views that people can have about those issues. Group discussion produces insights that can be more revealing than the data obtained from surveys or individual interviews. Thus they can indicate the range and depth of problems that might have to be solved and the future direction of policy. To use focus groups it is necessary:

- to ensure that a sufficient number of groups are convened with reasonably representative membership to provide a good cross section of opinion;
- to be clear about the purpose of the focus groups;
- to define the main issue to be considered;
- to prepare no more than half a dozen or so unequivocal questions that will generate discussion on an aspect of the main issue;
- for the convenor of each group to be able to pose and to clarify the questions, to encourage interaction, to control the discussion without being invasive and to sum up any conclusions reached or at least the main points made;
- to recognize that a focus group will not necessarily produce definitive views but should at least provide some indication of how people feel;
- to sum up the findings of the focus groups with conclusions on the policy implications.

Workshops

Workshops are often the best approach to involving people so that they not only interact together to form opinions but also jointly work out agreed conclusions about what needs to be done.

Definition

A workshop involves gathering a representative group of people to work together in analysing reward arrangements and requirements, discussing possible courses of action and, it is hoped, jointly deciding on the way forward. It is an exercise in participation designed to achieve agreed results as the basis for a development programme that might be managed by a project team.

Operation

Workshops are led by a facilitator, sometimes from within the organization, sometimes an outside consultant. The numbers of participants are ideally restricted to no more than 12 to encourage all involved to join in the proceedings. A workshop programme lasts half a day, at most a whole day, and typically consists of an introduction designed to set the scene by explaining the purpose of the workshop, what it will contain and how it will run. This is followed by one or more exercises designed to initiate focused discussion. The exercises have to be carefully chosen and designed to cover the key points. In a final session the conclusions reached during the workshop are summarized and the next steps agreed.

A workshop might only have one major exercise lasting over a morning as described below or it may include two or three exercises that progressively take the issue forward.

Conducting an exercise

A workshop built round one major exercise might use, for example, Figure 2.3 in Tool 2, which provides a means of analysing current reward practices. Statements could be added or deleted according to the situation and requirements of the organization, and the total number of statements could be reduced to cover key issues. The briefing by the facilitator to members of the workshop could be along the following lines:

- I am handing out a list of statements about reward policy and practice in this organization.
- Would each of you please look at each statement, for example 'People are fairly rewarded according to their contribution', and indicate individually on the form the extent to which you agree or disagree with the statement. Think about the reasons for your decision and make a brief note of this in the comments section.
- I will then divide you into three groups of four and ask each group to discuss a selection of the statements.
- Your aim should be to reach agreement on the statement and the reasons for it if you can, but if this is impossible please note the various views and reasons.
- Where you have come to a conclusion on each statement, please examine any which indicate that changes are required to the present arrangements and discuss and if possible agree on what should be done about it.
- I will then ask each group to present its findings to the whole workshop and we will discuss and, hopefully, agree on an agenda for future action.

A similar approach could be adopted when there is more than one exercise, although the scope for group discussion might be more limited, and such discussions can form the most valuable part of the exercise.

Another approach is to set up a design 'conclave'. This works best where the group involves key opinion formers and decision makers. It takes the form of an intensive workshop over two to three days and involves taking an issue through from initial principles to developed conclusions. It is useful where rapid progress needs to be made on an issue, or where decision makers are geographically dispersed and it is difficult otherwise to get people together for regular meetings. If rapid progress is to be made, the number of participants should be limited (eg up to 10) and roles need to be assigned, including record keeper and at least one person to draft outputs as they emerge.

Most of the instruments contained in the tools can be used as exercises. As noted earlier, a selection of these can be made or the instruments can be amended to suit the particular requirements of the workshop. Examples of how three exercises can be used are given below.

Rating reward strategy goals The rating framework shown in Tool 2 (Figure 2.9) can be used to obtain overall views and generate discussion on reward strategy.

The common goals (and any other relevant ones) can be rated by workshop participants in accordance with their views on how relatively important they are and the effectiveness (or ineffectiveness) of their current delivery. The aim is to start the process of defining and drafting specific objectives and priorities for reward. Quite often there will be low effectiveness scores given on some of the most important objectives, while individuals may differ on what they see as important goals. This exercise can be also used as the basis for a group discussion on what the key reward goals and priorities for the organization should be.

Gap analysis A gap analysis to compare the current and desired reward characteristics in the organization can be conducted using the framework set out in Figure 0.2. It involves comparing and contrasting what are thought to be the critical goals and choices in the organization, such as adopting a high or low stance in the external marketplace, or operating consistent policies in the organization versus varying practices in different parts of it. Respondents are asked to indicate the current emphasis in reward arrangements on the variables shown, and any others that may be relevant. They are then asked to indicate the desirable position. Comparing the largest gaps with the current situation helps to indicate the priority issues to be addressed.

Participants can discuss the grid together during the workshop or be asked to complete the grid individually in advance, indicating where in their view the emphasis should be on reward policies. Their average scores are plotted and the group can then review the findings and discuss the priorities they highlight. What is important is not whether the group achieves mathematical precision in where they plot each dimension, but the direction of change that is indicated from the discussion.

FIGURE 0.2   Example of a reward gap analysis in a pharmaceutical company

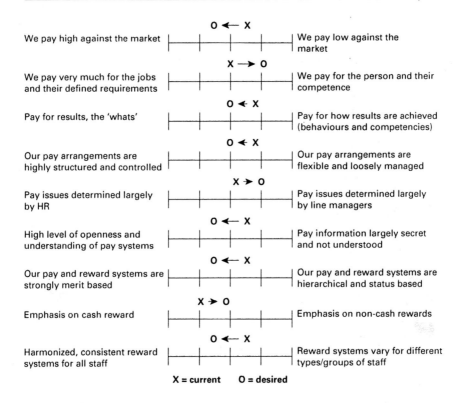

An example of a gap analysis conducted in a pharmaceutical company is shown in Figure 0.2. The plot shown averages the scores given by managers. Here it can be seen that there is general support amongst them for rewards in future to reflect better the skills and competencies of staff and their performance, greater consistency of approach across the organization and improved reward communications and understanding.

Total reward analysis Figure 0.3 is an example of analysing the total rewards strategy in a public sector organization using the Towers Perrin total rewards model. Workshop members were asked to describe the current total rewards provision using this grid. They were then asked to describe the improvements and changes in content and emphases they would like to see to better support the business of the organization, and make it a more rewarding and motivating place to work.

FIGURE 0.3 Current and required reward strategy

PAY	BENEFITS
Now	**Now**
• secure	• family-friendly
• below average	• paternalistic
• 'one size fits all'	• secure
Future	**Future**
• aligned to business goals	• individually tailored
• market rates	• flexibility
• flexible	• valued by employees
LEARNING	**ENVIRONMENT**
Now	**Now**
• good learning opportunities	• comfortable
• spoon-fed	• family
• structures	• formal
Future	**Future**
• more targeted training	• challenging
• focused on business goals	• responsive
• good opportunities as before	• enjoyable

Facilitating a workshop

The facilitator of a workshop has a vital role to play in ensuring that the workshop is effective. It is necessary to decide what role the facilitator is to play:

- *Hands off*: ie enabling the group to make their own decisions, through being observational and independent.
- *Collaborative*: supporting and being part of the group's decision making, characterized by engaging in the discussion whilst being inclusive and supportive of contributions from the whole group.
- *Directive*: providing information input, being consultative and taking positive control of moving the agenda on and decision making.

Whichever role is taken it is also necessary to:

- *Build rapport*: create a harmonious and understanding relationship in which everyone is at ease. This is done by gaining an understanding of how the workshop group is functioning and the issues with which its members are concerned and by 'matching' the language and behaviour of participants.
- *Set the scene*: ensure that everyone knows why the workshop has assembled and getting them to develop ground rules on how it should function.
- *Manage progress*: help the workshop members to agree what it is they are to achieve, review progress with them from time to time and summarize what has been achieved, making suggestions for the workshop to consider on future directions.

- *Control with a light touch*: act as a calming influence if the discussion gets too heated.
- *Get everyone involved*: ensure that everyone in the workshop has the opportunity to have a say without allowing anyone to hog the discussion.
- *Actively listen*: give people your full attention, reflect back to them what they have said and make it clear that what they are saying and their point of view are understood.
- *Ask questions*: create better understanding of the situation and encourage members of the workshop to think through the issues by asking for information on the factors involved.
- Be non-judgemental: not making adverse or critical comments on contributions from members of the group; elicit the facts and allow them to speak for themselves.

Project teams

The function of project teams (also known as task forces or working groups) is to achieve a purpose as defined in a brief. Reward management project teams are set up to develop and guide the implementation of a reward initiative such as a performance pay scheme. They may also be involved in conducting reward reviews and evaluating reward effectiveness. Teams should not be too large (maximum 10).

Ideally, project teams should provide a means of involvement in the planning and implementation of reward initiatives so that employees and their representatives have a voice in their design and operation. In such cases membership should consist of a representative number of stakeholders (eg line managers, other staff and trade unions). However, project teams can be composed entirely of management representatives and are therefore not part of an involvement exercise except in a more limited sense.

Whether they involve employees or are an instrument to achieve what management wants to do, project teams exist to manage projects using project management techniques as described below. However, even in the latter case, the team should take account of the views of employees and be prepared to initiate consultative processes to examine key issues that affect their interests. The team must also be prepared to plan and manage a communication programme to keep everyone informed of what is emerging from their deliberations.

Project management techniques

- Specify objectives, deliverables and success criteria.
- Carry out cost–benefit analysis or investment appraisal to justify project.

- Determine:
    - what should be done: the end result of the project;
    - who does what;
    - when it should be done (broken down into stages);
    - how much it should cost.
- Define resource requirements (people, money, etc).
- Prepare programme: identify stages.
- Define methods of control: charts, progress reports, progress (milestone) meetings.
- Identify, log and monitor risks.
- Ensure that everyone knows what is expected of them and is given the opportunity to express their views on what is being developed and how the project is progressing.
- Monitor progress continuously against the plan as well as at formal meetings.
- Take corrective action as required; for example, setting different priorities, reallocating resources.
- Evaluate the end result against the objectives and deliverables.

References

Armstrong, M and Brown, D (2006) *Strategic Reward*, Kogan Page, London

Purcell, J, Kinnie, K, Hutchinson, S, Rayton, B and Swart, J (2003) *People and Performance: How People Management Impacts on Organisational Performance*, CIPD, London

Tool 01
Reward reviews

Introduction

Reward reviews (sometimes referred to as audits) identify and assess what is being done about reward: internally in the shape of reward policies and practices, and externally by reference to evidence on reward and wider trends and developments. The outcome of a review might be the realization that a reward strategy (see Tool 2) or total rewards framework (see Tool 3) needs to be developed, or simply to focus on specific areas of reward. In either case a reward review should confirm the direction of change and the guiding principles for design and implementation.

Purpose of the tool

Reward management is a demanding and constantly evolving process. It is necessary to ensure that it is functioning well and this involves reviewing the policies and practices involved and taking steps to ensure that they operate effectively now and in the future. This tool describes the actions required to conduct a review and to make use of its findings. It is set out under the following headings:

- The reward review process;
- Conducting the review;
- Conclusions, recommendations and action planning.

The reward review process

The process of conducting a reward review is shown in Figure 1.1. It involves:

- researching and gathering both quantitative and qualitative information and evidence on existing reward policies and practices from inside the organization;
- gathering information on external reward practices, levels and trends; this can be used to assess the competitiveness and distinctiveness of rewards in the organization, as well as drawing out learning from relevant organizations externally, and from external research on specific reward practices;
- using this information to make assessments of the effectiveness of the delivery of reward goals and of the various pay and reward practices;
- thereby agreeing key reward issues to address;
- considering possible options and changes to improve the delivery of the reward goals;
- agreeing the reward changes required to improve effectiveness and planning their implementation;

FIGURE 1.1   The reward review process

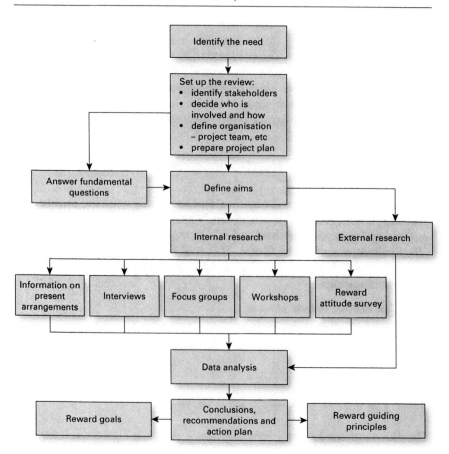

- deciding on the priorities, timescale and process for taking forward the results of the review.

Identify the need

It is necessary to identify the need for a review to provide guidance on how to proceed. Possible needs can be established by completing the questionnaire shown in Figure 1.2.

FIGURE 1.2 Questionnaire: identifying the need for a reward review

Possible factor	Tick if relevant	Circumstances to be taken into consideration
Changes in the external environment, eg legislation, sector regulations, product, competition or labour market changes, public perception		
Changes in the internal environment such as organization restructuring, the appointment of a new chief executive or HR director, the development of new business strategies, or the gathering of new information, for example on customers' views		
A major problem or crisis in relation to one specific aspect of reward, such as an inability to recruit or retain staff in a part of the organization, a significant funding issue in respect of a pension plan, an equal pay claim, poor employee relations, negative responses from employee attitude surveys		
Evidence that managers and/ or staff do not understand or appreciate aspects of their rewards, for example a low take up of choices within a flexible benefits plan, or common ignorance of an aspect of the employment package		
Others		

FIGURE 1.3   Questionnaire: setting up a reward review

Question	Answer
1 Who are the stakeholders, eg: • the board or trustees • top management team • senior managers, middle managers and supervisors • other staff, union or staff representatives • members or volunteers • third party providers of outsourced services?	
2 Which of those stakeholders should be involved in the review?	
3 How should they be involved, eg members of steering groups or project teams/task forces, focus groups, individual interviews, workshops, attitude surveys?	
4 Who should be responsible for leading and coordinating the review?	
5 Have we the expertise within the organization to conduct the review?	
6 Who might be involved in the review from within the organization as members of a project team, with or without outside help?	
7 If those who might be involved lack sufficient expertise, what training could be given to equip them for a task, either as leaders of the review without outside help or as participants if outside help is used?	
8 Do we need outside help from management consultants or other organizations such as pay/employment research or academic research bodies?	
9 If so, what would be their role? For example: taking full responsibility for conducting the review in conjunction with us; providing continuous or regular advice and services as required to our own project team; being available when required to provide advice or services?	
10 In the light of the answer to question 9, what sort of external support do we want, eg a large well-established general firm or organization, a large firm specialising in reward, a boutique firm specialising in reward, a sole practitioner specialising in reward?	
11 How do we organize the review, eg by the use of steering groups, project teams or task forces? What would be the membership and terms of reference of any group?	
12 What is our project plan?	

Set up the review

The questions to be answered in setting up a review are given in Figure 1.3.

Answer fundamental questions

The fundamental questions set out in Figure 1.4 can be used to assist in defining the aims of the review.

FIGURE 1.4   Fundamental review questions

Question	Answer
What are we trying to do here?	
What's important to this organization?	
How do we measure that?	
How are current reward practices helping or hindering what we are trying to do and what evidence do we have of this?	
How well is reward aligned to the purpose of the organization and the needs of its employees?	
Are we clear about what our primary reward goals are?	
Do we have clear guiding principles for reward?	
Do current reward policies and practices reflect our current and future staffing model?	
What evidence do we have to assess the current level of effectiveness and to highlight the strongest and weakest aspects of the current rewards package?	
What information can we gather to inform that review and how do we relate financial and non-financial information in making any assessment?	

Define aims

The aims of a reward review can be defined following discussions with stakeholders using the questionnaire shown in Figure 1.5.

FIGURE 1.5   Questionnaire: aims of a reward review

Possible aim	Comments on relevance and wording
Ensure that reward practices are supporting the achievement of corporate goals and satisfying the needs of stakeholders.	
Find out how well-established reward policies and practices are working and identify any problems.	
Establish whether reward innovations are functioning as planned and achieving the objectives set for them.	
Provide the evidence by means of internal research required to indicate what needs to be done to improve reward effectiveness.	
Identify good practice elsewhere by means of external research and note the lessons from research as a basis for examining the effectiveness of current reward activities.	
Ensure that value for money is obtained from the different parts of the reward system.	

Conducting the review

Having decided who will be involved in the review and its primary purpose, the fact finding and research can start. This consists of internal and external research and analysis of the data provided by the research to provide the basis for conclusions and recommendations. It also covers the important issues affecting line management responsibility for reward.

Internal research

Internal research aims to produce the evidence required to measure and analyse the effectiveness of reward. As described below, it starts by gathering information on present reward policies and practices and on how the responsibility for reward is allocated. This is supplemented by collecting data, views and suggestions by means of individual interviews, focus groups and workshops, and obtaining information on opinions and attitudes by means of surveys.

FIGURE 1.6   Checklist: background information

Area	Information	Reward implications
Organization	What are the key performance goals? How do staff contribute to their achievement? What skills are critical to our success? What performance information will be in place?	How strongly should pay and performance be linked? Do we want to reward skills development? Should we reward high levels of customer service?
Structure	How hierarchical and segmented? How important is flexibility/ multi-skilling? What is the nature of teamwork? How much mobility is there across the organization?	How much differentiation between the pay of individuals do we need? Should we reward teams? Should we reward flexibility/ multi-skilling? Should we segment rewards for different types of staff?
Culture and deal	What are our core values? What are the characteristic behavioural norms? What is the prevailing management style? What do we offer to employees and what do we expect in return?	How should we reinforce and reward our core values? Should we focus on recognition? How much freedom should managers have in rewarding their staff?
Employee needs	What is the profile of our employees – age, skills, status, etc? What are their primary motivations?	What rewards should we offer that appeal to this population? How much choice in the package should there be? What rewards (financial and non-financial) will attract and retain them?

Information on present reward policies and practices

Obtaining information on present arrangements involves a general review of the factors currently affecting reward (Figure 1.6) and against this background:

- obtaining data on reward policies and practices (Figure 1.7);
- considering the messages given by existing reward programmes (Figure 1.8).

FIGURE 1.7   Checklist: reward arrangements

Reward area	Points to be covered
Reward strategy	Is there a recognized reward strategy linked to the organization's goals and employee needs?
Reward policy	Are there clear and well-communicated policies on key aspects of reward, eg market stance?
Total reward	What steps have been taken to install and maintain a total reward approach?
Job evaluation	What job evaluation approach is in place? Does it facilitate the design and management of an equitable pay structure? Is it in line with the organization's values? Is there any evidence that the scheme has decayed, eg by allowing grade drift?
Equal pay	Has an equal pay survey been carried out? Is the organization vulnerable to an equal pay claim?
Base pay management	Are pay levels competitive? What type of grade and pay structures does the organization have for different groups?
	Are the structures appropriate to the business's culture and organization and the different groups? Is the structure flexible enough to cater for different needs?
	Are the grades/levels clearly defined?
	Are there too many grades or levels?
	What is the distribution of pay in different grades? To what extent does this conform to policy guidelines?
	Is there sufficient scope for pay progression?
	Is the structure reasonably easy to manage?
Pay progression	What is the basis for pay progression within the structure, eg performance or service?
	Do pay progression arrangements vary for different employee groups; if so, how?
	Are the arrangements for pay progression for different groups fair, equitable, consistent and transparent?
Bonuses	What bonus schemes are in place for different groups?
	To what extent do the schemes fairly and appropriately reward achievement and effort?
	Are bonus schemes funded by improved performance?
Employee benefits and pensions	What benefits are provided for different groups and are they appropriate?
	What are the pension arrangements and what changes, if any, are required or contemplated?
	Is there a flexible benefits scheme; if so, how does it work and what is the take up?
	Are employees aware of the value of their total remuneration?
Annual pay reviews	How are pay reviews (general and individual) conducted and how well run are they?
Communications	How well are reward policies and practices communicated to employees?
Reward evaluation	Is any attempt made to evaluate reward, if so how?
Value for money	What evidence is there that the organization is getting value for money from its reward practices?

FIGURE 1.8   Questionnaire: what messages do our pay programmes give?

Current reward policy or practice	What message does this policy or practice send?	What is the desired message?	How big is the gap?

Responsibility for reward

It is important to establish the extent to which line managers have the responsibility for making reward decisions and how well they are qualified to do so as the basis for deciding on the extent to which responsibility can be devolved by HR and the need for training and guidance to line managers on exercising their responsibility. A questionnaire modelled on the one shown in Figure 1.9 can be used for this purpose.

Individual interviews

An interview guide for senior executives is illustrated in Figure 1.10 and a checklist for interviewing line managers is given in Figure 1.11.

Focus groups

An example of an agenda for a focus group is given in Figure 1.12.

Workshops

Workshops consisting of employees and their representatives, line managers or a combination of these can be used to discuss views on reward arrangements using questions such as those given in Figures 1.10, 1.11 and 1.12. They can analyse the outcomes from interviews and focus groups and, as described below, attitude surveys. Workshops are an important means of involving employees in the review and evaluation of how the reward system works and in discussing innovations.

Reward attitude survey

Attitude surveys can be used to obtain more comprehensive information on the views of employees about the reward system. The requirements for a successful survey are set out in the introduction to this book. An example of a concise reward survey is given in Figure 1.13.

FIGURE 1.9 Questionnaire: responsibility for reward

Area of responsibility	Extent of responsibility for decisions			Extent to which line managers are qualified to exercise responsibility		
	Complete responsibility without reference to HR	*Subject to agreement of HR*	*Decisions entirely the responsibility of HR*	*Fully qualified*	*Partially qualified*	*Unqualified*
Deciding rates of pay on appointment, promotion or transfer						
Conducting pay reviews and deciding on individual pay increases						
Deciding on the grading or upgrading of staff						

FIGURE 1.10   Interview guide: senior executives

Area	Points to be covered
Purpose	Help to ensure alignment of rewards with the strategic direction of the organization.
	Consider need for and nature of reward review and changes.
	Give senior managers opportunity to input and shape the work.
Business/ organization	Key strategic goals and priorities.
	Brief outline of areas of responsibility, key goals, work flows and performance measures.
Current rewards	Strengths and weaknesses of current reward and recognition arrangements.
	External market definition – where staff are sourced and where they are lost to.
	Desired and actual levels of market competitiveness and any problem areas.
	Appropriateness and fairness of current internal relativities.
	Pay review process – strengths and weaknesses.
	Bonuses and incentives – types, levels, strengths and weaknesses.
	Other elements of the reward package – types, levels, strengths and weaknesses.
	Formal and informal recognition – how and how well it is done.
	Reward communications – how well and how attractively is the organization's employment brand communicated externally and how well is what the organization offers in the shape of total rewards communicated internally?
	How well do line managers manage and communicate reward?
	Levels of staff engagement and morale by level and function.
	Main motivators and demotivators.
Summary	Reward and recognition strengths, weaknesses and needs.
	Desirable and possible reward changes.
	What should be expected from a full reward review and who should be involved?

External research

The aim of external research is to obtain information about environmental factors, competitive pay levels, good practice in other organizations and lessons from research that can be used to indicate areas for action within the organization and to assess the effectiveness of current reward practices. A checklist of areas to be covered is given in Figure 1.14.

FIGURE 1.11   Questionnaire: line managers

Question	Response
1 To what extent do you understand the reward arrangements?	
2 To what extent are you able to explain the reward arrangements to your team?	
3 How much do the reward arrangements help or hinder you to carry out your job as a manager?	
4 Could you summarize your view of the reward arrangements in one sentence?	
5 How much authority have you to make reward decisions?	
6 How fairly does our reward system work?	
7 To what extent do you think people are rewarded appropriately according to their contribution?	
8 To what extent do you think our rates of pay are competitive?	
9 What do you believe your staff think of the reward system?	
10 Are there any changes you would like to see in the reward arrangements?	

FIGURE 1.12   Focus group agenda

Question	Response
What is good about the reward arrangements in the organization?	
What reward arrangements could be improved?	
Do you think people are rewarded appropriately for what they do?	
How well do reward levels compare with what could be earned elsewhere?	
How fairly do you think the organization's reward system operates?	
Would you like to see any changes in the reward arrangements?	

FIGURE 1.13 A reward attitude survey

Reward attitude survey
Please place a tick in the box that most closely fits your opinion

I believe that:	Strongly agree	Inclined to agree	Neither agree nor disagree	Inclined to disagree	Strongly disagree
1	My pay adequately rewards me for my contribution.					
2	The pay system is clear and easy to understand.					
3	It is right for staff to be rewarded according to their contribution.					
4	The basis upon which my pay is determined is fair.					
5	I am paid fairly compared with other jobs in the organization.					
6	Rates of pay in the organization are not consistent with levels of responsibility.					
7	My rate of pay compares favourably with rates paid outside the organization.					
8	My pay does not reflect my performance.					
9	The current pay system encourages better performance.					
10	The pay system badly needs to be reviewed.					

FIGURE 1.14   Checklist: areas for external research

- Studies of the changing labour market, in particular, the demand for and supply of key employee categories.
- Relevant legislation and regulatory frameworks, eg sector specific.
- Market rate surveys and analysis to assess the organization's competitive position.
- Benchmarking reward practices in comparable organizations.
- Reviews of studies on the reward strategies used by high-performing organizations.
- A review of external research studies conducted by academics, consultancies and organizations such as the Chartered Institute of Personnel and Development, The Institute for Employments Studies, E-Reward, IDS (Income Data Services) and IRS (Industrial Relations Review) regarding the effectiveness of reward practices and the conditions that make them more or less effective.

Data analysis

Data analysis can be carried out by means of a summary of the key issues raised by the internal and external research (Figure 1.15), a more specific analysis of the effectiveness of reward policies, design and processes (Figure 1.16) and a gap analysis (Figure 1.17).

FIGURE 1.15   Checklist: key reward issues

Type of issue	Evidence on the issue from the research
Dissatisfaction with the reward system with regard to such issues as fairness, equity, transparency and competitiveness	
Particular aspects of the reward system such as job evaluation, base pay management, contingent pay, bonuses, the benefits system, pensions and the administration of pay reviews are not working satisfactorily.	
The need for specific changes to any of the above aspects of reward has been identified.	
The reward system is not providing value for money.	
The reward system is difficult to manage.	
Others	

FIGURE 1.16 Questionnaire: reward effectiveness

Reward policies	Do they reinforce the achievement of business goals? Do they deliver value for money? Are they integrated with the HR strategy? What's the return on our reward spend?
Reward designs	Are they fit for purpose? Are they coherent/integrated? How do they compare with the market to recruit and retain? Do they meet the needs of different employees? How do cost and perceived value compare?
Reward processes	How well implemented/operated are they? How well communicated? How effective are line managers? What's the employees' experience of them?

FIGURE 1.17 Questionnaire: reward gap analysis

What should be happening?	What is happening?	What needs to be done?
1 A total reward approach is adopted that emphasizes the significance of both financial and non-financial rewards.		
2 Reward policies and practices are developed within the framework of a well-articulated strategy that is designed to support the achievement of business objectives and meet the needs of stakeholders.		
3 A job evaluation scheme is used that properly reflects the values of the organization, is up-to-date with regard to the jobs it covers and is non-discriminatory.		
4 Equal pay issues are given serious attention. This includes the conduct of equal pay reviews that lead to action.		
5 Market rates are tracked carefully so that a competitive pay structure exists that contributes to the attraction and retention of high quality people.		
6 Grade and pay structures are based on job evaluation and market rate analysis, are appropriate to the characteristics and needs of the organization and its employees, facilitate the management of relativities, provide scope for rewarding contribution, clarify reward and career opportunities, are constructed logically, operate transparently and are easy to manage.		

FIGURE 1.17   *Continued*

What should be happening?	What is happening?	What needs to be done?
7 Contingent pay schemes reward contribution fairly and consistently, support the engagement of staff and the development of a performance culture, deliver the right messages about core values, contain a clear 'line of sight' between contribution and reward and are cost effective.		
8 Performance management processes contribute to performance improvement, people development and the management of expectations, operate effectively throughout the organization and are supported by line managers and staff.		
9 Employee benefits and pension schemes meet the needs of stakeholders and are cost effective.		
10 A flexible benefits approach is adopted.		
11 Reward management procedures exist that ensure that reward processes are managed effectively and that costs are controlled.		
12 Appropriate use is made of technology to assist in the process of reward management and its communication.		
13 Reward management aims and arrangements are transparent and communicated well to staff.		
14 Surveys are used to assess the opinions of staff about reward and action is taken on the outcomes.		
15 An appropriate amount of responsibility for reward is devolved to line managers.		
16 Line managers are capable of carrying out their devolved responsibilities well.		
17 Steps are taken to train line managers and provide them with support and guidance as required.		
18 HR has the knowledge and skills to provide the required reward management advice and services and to guide and support line managers.		
19 Reward management developments are affordable and cost effective.		
20 Steps are taken to evaluate the effectiveness of reward management processes.		

Conclusions, recommendations and action planning

The conclusions, recommendations and action plans should be prepared in conjunction with stakeholders and then communicated to them. It is particularly important to prepare a comprehensive and realistic action plan for further design work and implementation. The questions to be answered when preparing the plan are set out in Figure 1.18

FIGURE 1.18 Questionnaire: action planning

Action plan questions	Action plan answers
What needs to be done?	
Why does it need to be done?	
How will it affect employees?	
What benefits will it provide in terms of a positive impact on business performance and employee engagement?	
How much will it cost?	
How will it be done?	
Who will do it?	
When will it be done?	

Tool 02
Reward strategy

Introduction

A reward strategy provides a business- and people-focused description of what the organization wants to do about reward over the next few years and how it intends to do it. The need for a reward strategy may be identified from a review of the current reward arrangements and situation as described in Tool 1. The aim of reward strategy is to provide the organization with a sense of purpose and direction in delivering reward programmes that support the achievement of business and HR goals and meet the needs of stakeholders. It defines pathways that link the needs of the business and its people with the reward policies and practices of the organization and thereby communicates and explain these practices.

All reward strategies are different, just as all organizations are different. Of course, similar aspects of reward will be covered in the strategies of different organizations but they will be treated differently in accordance with variations between organizations in their contexts, business strategies and cultures. But the reality of reward strategy is that it is not such a clear-cut process as some believe. It evolves, it changes and it has sometimes to be reactive rather than proactive.

Purpose of the tool

A systematic approach to analysing the context and needs, assessing the alternatives available and deciding what approach to adopt to implementation is desirable, and this tool aims to provide the framework and means for making such an approach. It contains a series of questionnaires and checklists covering the actions set out in Figure 2.1 required to develop and implement reward strategies. In doing so it takes account of the employer perspective and that of the employee.

FIGURE 2.1 The reward strategy development framework

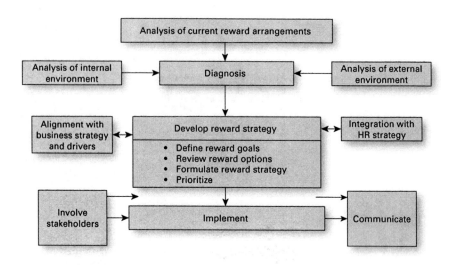

Contents of the tool

This tool covers:

- Analysis of reward strategy and practices;
- Environment analysis;
- Diagnosis;
- Developing and implementing reward strategy.

FIGURE 2.2 Analysis of existing reward strategy

The reward strategy:	In full	Mostly	Partly	Not at all
Is aligned to business strategy.				
Has clearly defined goals based on business objectives.				
Well-articulated guiding principles exist.				
Provides a framework for reward decisions.				
Is long term.				
Is flexible enough to change when circumstances require.				

Analysis of reward strategy and practices

The analysis of current reward strategy and practices is the starting point. It is carried out through a reward review as described in Tool 1. Conclusions can be summarized in Figure 2.2 for reward strategy and Figure 2.3 for reward practices. A detailed analysis of the gap between what is required and what is happening and the actions than need to be taken to fill the gap can be analysed.

FIGURE 2.3   Analysis of current reward practices

Statement	Fully agree	Partly agree	Partly disagree	Fully disagree	Comments
1 We have well defined and understood reward guiding principles.					
2 Our reward system effectively enhances the engagement of people.					
3 We implement our policy on levels of pay compared with market rates.					
4 We pay insufficient attention to non-financial rewards.					
5 We are satisfied with our methods of deciding on internal relativities.					
6 There is an unacceptable incidence of grade drift (unjustified upgradings).					
7 We are vulnerable to an equal pay claim.					
8 Our rates of pay are uncompetitive.					
9 We do not have adequate data on market rates.					
10 We have too many grades in our pay structure.					

FIGURE 2.3 *Continued*

Statement	Fully agree	Partly agree	Partly disagree	Fully disagree	Comments
11 Our grade structure is too complex.					
12 People are fairly rewarded according to their contribution.					
13 Our reward system does not succeed in motivating people.					
14 Our reward system helps to attract and retain high-quality people.					
15 We get value for money from our reward system.					
16 Our performance management processes work well.					
17 We have an excellent and competitive range of employee benefits.					
18 There is room for more choice by employees on benefits.					
19 We spend too much on employee benefits.					
20 Our pension scheme is too expensive.					

Environment analysis

Reward strategy will be contingent on the internal and external environments. These can be analysed using Figures 2.4 and 2.5 as the framework for that purpose.

Diagnosis

Following the analysis, the emerging issues and the reasons for them can be analysed as a basis for action using the diagnostic framework set out in Figure 2.6.

FIGURE 2.4   Analysis of internal environment

Question	Response	Implications for reward strategy
What are the key objectives of our business strategy?		
What are the main drivers of success in our business?		
What are the core values of the organization?		
What evidence is there that these values are used in the everyday life of the organization?		
What are the implications for our reward strategy of the type of business we are in?		
To what extent do we manage centrally or devolve responsibility?		
What is it like to work for this organization?		
What characteristics do we look for in our people?		
What do the people we want, want?		
What is our employee value proposition and does it help to attract and retain high-quality people?		
What do we do to ensure the engagement of our people, and is it enough?		

If the reward and goals have not already been identified through a reward review (see Tool 1), they need to be confirmed before embarking on detailed design.

Developing and implementing reward strategy

The formulation of reward strategy can be described as a process for developing a sense of direction and making the best use of resources. The steps required to develop it are:

1 Ensure that the reward strategy supports the achievement of the business and HR strategies by considering the implications of the business strategy and how integration can be achieved (Figures 2.7 and 2.8).

FIGURE 2.5   Analysis of external environment

External factor	Impact on HR policy and practice	Impact on reward strategy
Competitive pressures		
Business/economic downturn		
Globalization		
Employment and demographic trends		
Legislation/regulations		
Availability of key skills		
Market rates of pay and trends		

FIGURE 2.6   Diagnostic framework

Issues identified by analysis	Reasons for issues	Action proposed to deal with issues

2 Define reward goals (Figure 2.9).

3 Review reward options in relation to reward goals and practicality (Figure 2.10).

4 Identify possible reward strategies within a framework (Figure 2.11).

5 Formulate strategy with reference to guidelines (Figure 2.12).

6 Prioritize the implementation of the strategy (Figure 2.13).

7 Plan implementation (Figure 2.14).

Stakeholders should be involved in all these steps as described in the Introduction to these tools. A communications strategy is required that keeps people informed of what is happening.

Step 1: Integrate

FIGURE 2.7 Implications for reward of business strategy

	Possible elements	Actual elements	Implications for reward strategy
Business strategy	Growth – revenue/profit Maximize shareholder value Growth through acquisitions/ mergers Growth in production/servicing facilities Product development Market development Price/cost leadership		
Business drivers	Innovation Maximize added value Productivity Customer service Quality Satisfy stakeholders – investors, employees, elected representatives Price/cost leadership		

FIGURE 2.8 Integration of HR and reward strategies

HR strategy area	Possible reward strategy contribution	Proposed action
Resourcing	Total reward approaches that help to make the organization a great place in which to work; competitive pay structures that help to attract and retain high-quality people	
Performance management	Contingent pay schemes that contribute to the motivation and engagement of people; performance management processes that promote continuous improvement and encourage people to uphold core values	

FIGURE 2.8 *Continued*

HR strategy area	Possible reward strategy contribution	Proposed action
Talent management	Non-financial rewards such as recognition and opportunities for growth and development; policies that recognize talented people for their contribution; career-linked grade and pay structure, for example a career family structure	
Learning and development	Performance management processes that identify learning needs and how they can be satisfied; career family structures that define career ladders in terms of knowledge and skill requirements	
Work environment	Total reward approaches that emphasize the importance of enhancing the work environment; work–life balance policies	

Step 2: Define reward goals

It is useful to agree reward goals at this stage against which proposed strategies can be assessed and the effectiveness of strategies in reaching these goals after implementation can be evaluated. Figure 2.9 contains a rating framework to help in deciding on the goals.

FIGURE 2.9 Rating framework for reward strategy goals

Goals	Importance*	Effectiveness*
Reinforce the achievement of organizational goals		
Recruit and retain staff of the required calibre		
Facilitate staff mobility		
Strong relationships between pay and performance		
Reinforce organizational values		
Motivating for employees		

FIGURE 2.9 *Continued*

Goals	Importance*	Effectiveness*
Cost effective		
Well communicated and understood by employees		
Managed effectively in practice by line managers		
Efficient to operate/maintain		
Flexible in order to react to change		
Others (list)		

* Scale: 10 = high; 1 = low

Step 3: Review reward options

A preliminary look at the reward options in relation to goals and their practicality can be undertaken with the help of the review framework set out in Figure 2.10. This can be used to test different design options.

FIGURE 2.10 Review of reward options in relation to reward goals and practicality

Change option	Goal A	Goal B	Goal C	Capacity – cost and resource to effect change	Competence – ease of implementation and operation	Commitment – employee and management support
Job evaluation – new analytical scheme	✓✓	✗	✓	✗✗	✗	?
Simplified job evaluation administration process	✓✓	✓	✓	✓	✓	✓✓
Grading – new single structure with fewer grades	✓	✓	✓	✗	✗	✗

Step 4: Identify possible reward strategies

The table in Figure 2.11 can be used to identify which reward approaches will best support the broader strategy.

FIGURE 2.11 Reward strategy formulation framework

Strategy area		Examples of possible solutions	Yes	No	Modify
Financial	Total reward	Introduce total reward approach			
	Job evaluation	Develop new analytical scheme			
		Develop new non-analytical scheme			
		Modify existing scheme			
		Rely on analytical matching			
	Grade and pay structure	Reduce number of grades considerably (broad grading)			
		Introduce broad banding			
		Develop job or career family structure			
		Replace pay spine			
	Contingent pay	Introduce performance-related pay (not pay spine)			
		Introduce contribution-related pay (not pay spine)			
		Introduce variable pay (bonus) scheme			
	Employee benefits	Revise benefits provision			
		Introduce flexible benefits			
	Pensions	Change to defined contribution scheme			
Non-financial	Recognition	Introduce formal recognition scheme			
	Scope for development and growth	Improve learning and development programmes			
	Autonomy	Encourage, guide and train line managers to increase autonomy			
	Working environment	Develop 'great place to work' policies			
	Work–life balance	Introduce more comprehensive work–life balance policies			

Step 5: Apply reward strategy guidelines

Use the guidelines set out in Figure 2.12 when formulating each strategy.

FIGURE 2.12 Guidelines for formulating reward strategies

To what extent does the reward strategy:	Answer
• support the business strategy?	
• support the HR strategy?	
• save clearly defined goals, success criteria and deliverables?	
• provide a clear basis for future action?	
• demonstrate that it can readily be implemented?	

Step 6: Prioritize

Figure 2.13 can be used to prioritize the changes that will support the overall reward strategy.

FIGURE 2.13 Prioritization of strategy development

Strategy area		Proposed strategy	Priority (1,2,3, etc)	Proposed programme	
				Start	Finish
Financial	Total reward				
	Job evaluation				
	Grade and pay structure				
	Contingent pay				
	Employee benefits				
	Pensions				
	Other				
Non-Financial	Recognition				
	Scope for development and growth				
	Autonomy				
	Working environment				
	Work–life balance				
	Other				

Step 7: Plan implementation

The fundamental principle of reward strategy development is to plan with implementation in mind. The only good strategy is one that works. But putting what seems to be a good idea into practice is often very difficult. The checklist in Figure 2.14 can be referred to when planning implementation.

FIGURE 2.14   Implementation checklist

Have you:	✔
• specified the objectives of the project, its success criteria and its deliverables?	
• defined who is to be responsible for directing and managing the project and the degree of authority they have?	
• set out what should be done (activities), who does what, and when it will be done?	
• involved senior managers/heads of department as sponsors, to provide comment, guidance, support and encouragement?	
• involved line managers and staff in the strategy development, planning and implementation programme?	
• communicated to all concerned the objectives of the programme, how it will take place and how they will be affected?	
• broken the project into stages with defined starting and completion dates to produce the programme?	
• clarified interdependencies?	
• defined resource requirements – people, outside advisors, finance?	
• defined methods of control and risk management, eg progress reports, meetings?	
• ensured that everyone knows what is expected of them and has the briefing, guidance and resources required?	
• seen that progress is monitored continuously against the plan as well as at formal meetings?	
• ensured that corrective action is taken as required, eg amending timings, reallocating resources?	
• evaluated progress and the end result against objectives, success criteria and deliverables?	

Communications accountability

It is necessary not only to decide on how information should be communicated as suggested in the Introduction to these tools, but also to decide who is accountable for what aspects of communication in respect of various aspects of the reward package. Figure 2.15 can be used to plot accountabilities.

FIGURE 2.15 Framework for plotting accountabilities for reward communications

Reward element	Senior management	Line manager	Human resources
Base pay objectives			
Base pay position			
Base pay progression			
Variable pay			
Benefits			

Tool 03
Total rewards

Introduction: the concept of total rewards

Total rewards is an approach to reward management that emphasizes the need to consider all aspects of the work experience of value to employees, not just a few such as pay and employee benefits. It aims to blend the financial and non-financial elements of reward into a cohesive whole.

The total rewards approach recognizes that it is necessary to get financial rewards (pay and benefits) right. But it also appreciates the importance of providing people with rewarding experiences that arise from the work they do, their work environment, how they are managed and the opportunity to develop their skills and careers. It contributes to the production of an employee value proposition that provides a clear, compelling reason why talented people should work for an organization. A total rewards model is set out in Figure 3.1.

FIGURE 3.1 The elements of total rewards

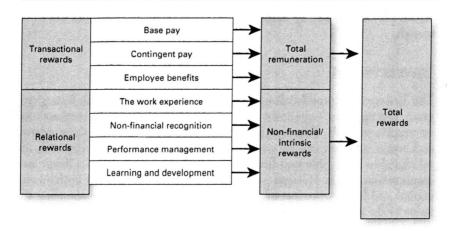

Purpose of the tool

The purpose of the tool is to describe how the abstract but compelling concept of total reward can be put into effect. This is not easy. It is not just a matter of introducing a recognition scheme in addition to conventional contingent pay systems. And it means going beyond simply tacking on to existing pay and employee benefit practices a number of established HR policies and processes – learning and development, job design, employee well-being and the like. What it should involve – and what this tool describes – is ensuring that a cohesive approach is taken to integrating the various approaches that are available to increase engagement.

Contents of the tool

This tool covers:

- Models of total rewards;
- Developing a total rewards approach.

Models of total rewards

A framework is required for the development of a total rewards approach, one that can be used as a basis for discussions with management and employees on what the concept means and what it looks like. One model is shown in Figure 3.1 above. A number of others have been produced, mainly by consultancies. Three of the most important models – the ones created by Towers Perrin, Zingheim and Schuster, and WorldatWork are described below. This is followed by a summary of the contents of those and five other models.

Towers Perrin

The Towers Perrin model shown in Figure 3.2 is a matrix with four quadrants. The upper two quadrants – pay and benefits – represent transactional or tangible rewards. These are financial in nature and are essential to recruit and retain staff but can be easily copied by competitors. By contrast, the relational or intangible non-financial rewards represented in the lower two quadrants cannot be imitated so readily and can therefore create both human capital and human process advantage. They are essential to enhancing the value of the upper two quadrants.

FIGURE 3.2 Towers Perrin total rewards model

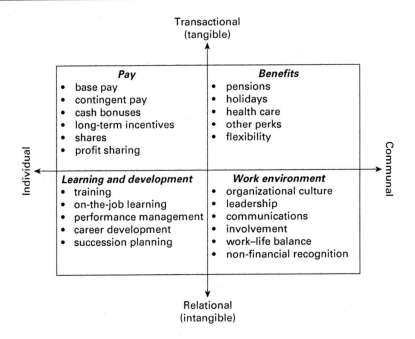

Transactional
(tangible)

Pay	**Benefits**
• base pay	• pensions
• contingent pay	• holidays
• cash bonuses	• health care
• long-term incentives	• other perks
• shares	• flexibility
• profit sharing	

Individual ←→ Communal

Learning and development	**Work environment**
• training	• organizational culture
• on-the-job learning	• leadership
• performance management	• communications
• career development	• involvement
• succession planning	• work–life balance
	• non-financial recognition

Relational
(intangible)

Zingheim and Schuster

The total rewards model developed by Zingheim and Schuster (2000) expresses total rewards as four interlocked and directly related components as shown in Figure 3.3.

FIGURE 3.3 Model of total rewards: Zingheim and Schuster

Individual growth	**Total pay**
• Investment in people	• Base pay
• Development and training	• Variable pay (cash and stock)
• Performance management	• Benefits or indirect pay
• Career enhancement	• Recognition and celebration
Compelling future	**Positive workplace**
• Vision and values	• People focus
• Company growth and success	• Leadership
• Company image and reputation	• Colleagues
• Stakeholdership	• Work itself
• Win–win over time	• Involvement
	• Trust and commitment
	• Open communications

FIGURE 3.4 Summary of elements in total rewards models

	Armstrong	Hay	IDS	Mercer	Sibson	Towers Watson	World atWork	Zinghem and Schuster
Financial rewards (general)		*	*	*	*		*	
Base pay	*	*				*		*
Contingent pay	*	*				*		*
Benefits	*	*		*		*	*	*
Career development			*	*	*	*	*	
Compelling future								*
Involvement						*	*	*
Leadership						*		*
Learning and development	*		*	*		*		*
Organizational culture			*			*		
People focus								*
Performance management	*					*	*	*
Recognition				*			*	*
Work environment and experience including the work itself	*		*		*	*		
Work–life balance			*	*		*	*	
Intangible reward		*						

WorldatWork

WorldatWork, formerly the American Compensation Association, introduced the concept of total rewards in the 1990s. Their first model was produced in 2000 and revised in 2006 (Christopherson and King, 2006).

The five elements of total rewards in the 2006 model are compensation, benefits, work–life balance, performance and recognition, and development and career opportunities. These are influenced by the external environment, the work experience, organizational culture and the business and HR strategies. The combined five elements facilitate the attraction, motivation and retention of employees, which enhances their satisfaction and engagement and impacts on business performance and results.

Summary of models

The elements included in the various models are summarized in Figure 3.4.

This summary shows, as might be expected, a common approach to financial rewards. There is a wider range of non-financial elements. The six most popular elements are:

- career development;
- learning and development;
- work–life balance;
- recognition;
- performance management;
- work environment and experience, including the work itself.

Introducing total rewards

The steps required to introduce total rewards are set out in Figure 3.5 and are discussed below.

Clarify the concept and objectives of total rewards

A programme for developing total rewards should start with a clarification of the meaning of the concept and its purposes in which stakeholders (senior management, line managers, employees and their representatives) should be involved. Statements of meaning and purpose provide the basis for further discussions with stakeholders, decisions on the elements of a total rewards programme and the preparation of a business case.

It is useful to generate discussions with management and employees about the meaning and purpose of total rewards before considering how the concept might be developed in detail. A forced-choice questionnaire can be used as set out in Figure 3.6.

FIGURE 3.5   Introducing total rewards

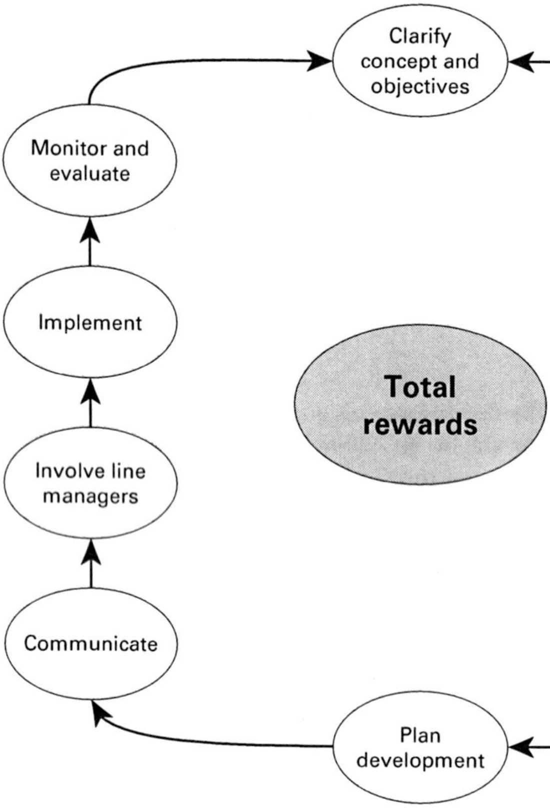

Involve stakeholders

Stakeholders should be involved as much as possible in developing total rewards. Their commitment to the programme will be enhanced if they can contribute their ideas at the initial stage when the broad features and aims of the concept are defined and thereafter when the elements of total rewards are selected and their introduction prioritized. An example of an executive questionnaire is given in Figure 3.7 and another example of an employee questionnaire that can be used to identify employee total reward priorities is provided in Figure 3.8.

Identify total reward elements

The identification of the total reward elements means, in effect, either adopting or adapting one of the existing total rewards models or developing a different model that suits the organization's needs. However, the latter will

FIGURE 3.6   Total rewards forced-choice questionnaire

Which of the following statements best describes the concept of total rewards?
- A combination of base pay and performance pay
- A combination of financial and non-financial rewards
- A combination of base pay, performance pay and employee benefits
- A combination of performance pay and a recognition scheme

The concept of total reward is:
- about issuing statements to employees setting out the total value of the pay and benefits they receive.
- synonymous with the concept of total remuneration.
- about ensuring that the provision of rewards takes account of all the factors that affect engagement and motivation.
- about ensuring that individuals are rewarded for their total contribution.

The concept of total rewards provides:
- a way of thinking about reward strategy.
- a means of achieving the integration of different financial reward practices.
- a means of ensuring that all aspects of reward are catered for.
- a method of conducting base pay management.

The purpose of a total rewards approach is to:
- ensure that value for money is obtained from the organization's reward practices.
- contribute to winning the full engagement of employees.
- help in the design of efficient reward systems.
- ensure that employees fully understand and appreciate the reward opportunities available to them.

A total rewards approach will:
- provide the flexibility required to cater for the fact that individuals have different wants and needs that affect their engagement and motivation.
- ensure that attention is given to the introduction of a recognition scheme.
- achieve a proper balance between financial and non-financial rewards.
- guarantee that employees will be more highly motivated.

undoubtedly include some of the non-financial elements contained in the published models as well, of course, the basic pay and benefits elements.

Basic approach

In its basic form, a total rewards approach means simply getting the financial reward elements right and consciously doing whatever is possible progressively to enhance the elements in the form of various HR practices that contribute to non-financial rewards.

The problem with this approach is that it could be unfocused. A specific approach that can be based on one of the total reward models will be better from the viewpoint of clarifying the concept and providing a basis for defining, developing and communicating its elements.

FIGURE 3.7 Executive interview questions for total rewards project

---

Business performance
- What aspects of performance in the company do you want to improve?
- What are the company's biggest anticipated challenges over the next three years?
- How will you differentiate yourself from competitors if you pursue these goals?
- What external changes are most important to the company? How are these changes affecting the company?
- How do you measure performance? What is your performance on these measures today? What needs to happen to improve these?
- Is there anything that is important to your strategic intent that you currently do not/cannot measure?
- What would the impact on the company be if:
  - One business area has higher labour costs than other areas but still achieves targets?
  - One business area meets financial targets – but fails to deliver on qualitative targets?
- How does the business planning cycle work?

People issues
- Where do you recruit from and how difficult is it to attract, retain and motivate people?
- Do you have any specific issues with respect to the composition of the reward package?
- Do you believe you have the right 'deal' with employees? If not, how does it need to change?
- How would you believe employees would define total rewards?
- What are your objectives with respect to costs: reduce, allocate differently, shift a proportion from fixed to variable?
- How competitive should the total package be? At competitive norm, above or below? Does this vary by employee group/business?
- In which area do you think better alignment would yield the greatest return: pay, benefits, learning and development, work environment? Are there barriers to greater alignment?
- Are there any lines that you would draw with respect to what should be applied on a common basis across the company and what should be differentiated?

Pay
- In the culture of the company, to what extent can employee performance be meaningfully enhanced through pay – does this vary by category of employee?
- To what extent should base pay be tied to competitive levels?
- What factors should play the greatest part in determining pay:
  - Values and behaviours?
  - Skills/knowledge/abilities?
  - Market rate?
  - Competitive behaviours?
  - Position in the hierarchy?
  - Experience/tenure?
  - Results?
- What is more important – to pay competitively against the market or to pay fairly relative to other employees – within the business/across the company?
- How much authority do managers have to make pay decisions?
- Is there value in extending the company's incentive plans beyond those currently covered?

FIGURE 3.7 *Continued*

Benefits
- Are there any aspects of the benefits package that you think should be changed – any that should not be touched?
- Are there any areas where you think the employee should have more choice in selecting benefits/remuneration elements?

Learning and development
- To what extent are learning and development an integral part of the deal in working at the company?
- Is sufficient emphasis placed on learning and development?

Work environment
- How important is the work environment compared with pay/benefits in attracting and retaining people – to what extent does it give you a competitive advantage?
- Are there any elements that you would change/leave untouched?

This project
- What do you think are the greatest barriers to change?
- At the conclusion of this project, what will success look like?

FIGURE 3.8 Employee total reward priorities

Assuming there are 100 points to distribute between the following aspects of your total reward package, distribute these points in terms of how important they are to you. You can allocate points to as many items as you like (up to a maximum of ...); eg if basic salary is the only aspect of reward that is important to you, allocate all 100 points to this.	
Aspect of employment	
A competitive base salary	10
Pension	9
Car allowance	8
Health benefits	10
Death in service cover	3
Permanent health insurance (prolonged disability cover)	8
Flexibility of working hours	10
Holidays	9
Identity with organization values	10
The leadership of the organization	2
Staff discounts	3

FIGURE 3.8 *Continued*

Stimulating and challenging work	3
Flexibility to deal with caring responsibilities	4
Working for an organization with a distinct and high profile	1
Access to fitness facilities	2
Learning and development opportunities	1
Encouraging a healthy lifestyle	2
Personal recognition (non-monetary)	1
Opportunities for career advancement	9
Other (please specify)	

Choice of elements

The core of any total rewards model will be pay and benefits but there is a choice on what other, non-financial, elements should be included. An analysis of the non-financial elements contained in the various models listed earlier shows that there are plenty to choose from. The choice is made more difficult because while some elements such as recognition, performance management, work–life balance and learning and development are clear cut, others such as the work environment are more diffuse.

There are four approaches that can be adopted:

- A deductive approach that means taking one of the models and seeing how well it applies. It may involve selecting the most appealing consultant's model on the grounds that it contains a more attractive portfolio of elements and/or because of the reputation of the consultancy.

- An inductive approach that means first collecting the views of employees and making sense of them, then interactively fitting these views with a model, and finally establishing and dealing with any gap between the positions of employees and management.

- Distil the existing models, benchmark the total reward experiences of other organizations and produce an individualized approach, for example: pay, benefits, recognition, career development, work–life balance, performance management and work environment. These could all be defined and programmes produced for their development.

- Add recognition or another element to pay and benefits as a starting point and bring in other elements as part of a longer-term strategic HR plan.

The criteria for choice would be the extent to which the element is appropriate, will benefit the organization and its employees in specific ways and can be implemented without too much difficulty.

Prioritize

It is best not to be too ambitious in introducing total rewards. Start by identifying 'win–win' initiatives – those that are likely to have a notable effect on employee engagement and can be developed without too much difficulty. If a comprehensive approach is envisaged, priorities will need to be established and the introduction of the less immediate elements phased. Examples of possible developments are:

- Revise grade and pay structure, possibly instituting a career family structure that defines career paths.
- Revise contingent pay scheme or develop new one. Include leadership and upholding core values as important factors in a contribution-related pay scheme.
- Introduce flexible benefits scheme.
- Issue total reward statements that spell out to employees the value of all the benefits they receive in addition to pay.
- Introduce a non-financial recognition scheme.
- Improve performance management system, including leadership and upholding core values as important factors.
- Enhance learning and development, talent management and career development programmes.
- Focus management development programmes on improving the ability of line managers to play a major part in providing relational rewards.
- Take steps to improve work–life balance.
- Educate line managers in the principles of job design and provide guidance to them on developing roles that provide for intrinsic motivation.

Make the business case for total rewards

It can be argued that total rewards can help to achieve one or more of the following:

- Promote a culture that values, recognizes and rewards outstanding performance.
- Achieve competitive advantage by offering levels of choice and personalization not provided by other employers competing for the same type of people.

- Meet varied and changing employee needs by introducing more value, choice and flexibility.
- Help to make the company an 'employer of choice' for people already employed there, as well as for potential recruits.
- Enhance employees' engagement and therefore performance.
- Ensure that the best use is made of all the possible ways of rewarding people, in combination as well as individually.
- Avoid dependence on dubious and expensive financial incentives.

Plan the development programme

Introducing total rewards in its fullest sense is not easy. WorldatWork (2000) commented that total rewards are 'simple in concept and, at best, complex in execution'. The transactional and tangible elements of total rewards (financial rewards) are quite clear cut. It may not be easy to make them work well but it is not too difficult to decide on what needs to be done. Recognition schemes that may be financial or non-financial (or a combination of the two) can be included in this category.

Relational or non-financial rewards are more difficult. It is not a matter of implementing quick-fix programmes. The organization can contribute by communicating the values, giving employees a voice, setting up performance management processes, and taking steps to improve work–life balance. A conscious effort can be made to 'bundle' reward and HR practices together, for example developing career family structures where the emphasis is on mapping career paths rather than providing a pay structure. Importantly, the organization can ensure that line managers appreciate the importance of using relational rewards – exercising effective leadership, giving feedback, recognizing achievement and providing meaningful work. Ultimately, relational rewards are in the hands of line managers, and what the organization must do is to ensure as far as possible that they understand the significance of this aspect of their work and are given the training and guidance needed to acquire the skills to do it well.

Communicate

The nature of the total rewards concept, how it will be introduced and managed and how people will benefit need to be communicated. Models can help. It is particularly important to communicate to line managers the importance of their role in implementing total rewards.

Total reward statements communicate to employees the value of the employee benefits that they receive in addition to their pay, such as pensions, holidays, company cars, free car parking and subsidized meals. They also describe any other rewards they get such as learning and development opportunities. The aim is to ensure that they appreciate the total value of their reward package.

Involve line managers

Line managers contribute to the management of total rewards in six important ways:

- They have considerable influence over the management of financial rewards, agreeing starting salaries and proposing pay increases and bonuses.
- The effectiveness of performance management as a reward process involving feedback and the initiation of individual learning and development programmes is mainly up to them.
- They are the most important elements in a recognition scheme – giving praise where praise is due, publicly acknowledging high performance and making recognition awards as provided for by the scheme.
- They strongly influence how jobs are designed and therefore the degree to which people are provided with intrinsic rewards from the work itself.
- They control the degree of work flexibility that can take place and therefore work–life balance.
- It is their qualities of leadership that largely contribute to the creation of a rewarding work environment.

This is why their involvement in the development of total rewards is vital. Management development and training programmes that define their role and increase their total reward management skills are also important.

Implement

Planning a total rewards programme may be hard; implementing it can be even more difficult. It is an exercise in change management: for employees generally when new reward practices are being introduced and for line managers in particular if they are expected to change their behaviour. Continuing communications and involvement of stakeholders are essential.

Monitor and evaluate

It is essential to monitor the implantation of total rewards carefully and then to evaluate how well each element has worked against the objectives set for it. This can lead to a reclarification of the concept and amendments to reward practices as required.

References

Armstrong, M (2010) *Handbook of Reward Management Practice*, 3rd edn, Kogan Page, London

Christopherson, J and King, B (2006) The 'it' factor: a new total rewards model leads the way, *WorldatWork Journal*, Fourth quarter, pp 18–19, 22, 24, 26–27

WorldatWork (2000) *Total Rewards: From Strategy to Implementation*, WorldatWork, Scottsdale, AZ

Zingheim, P K and Schuster, J E (2000) *Pay People Right! Breakthrough strategies to create great companies*, Jossey-Bass, San Francisco

Tool 04
Reward risk management

Introduction

Risk is inherent in every business activity that we undertake. The development, implementation and management of reward systems and processes are no exception. In recent years there have been plenty of examples of the damage that can be done by failing to manage the risks associated with remuneration decisions. This has been exemplified by some very public cases including rogue or mismanaged trading in the financial sector linked to incentive arrangements, and the alleged misuse of expenses by British parliamentarians. Notwithstanding potential external damage to brand or reputation, the mishandling of reward issues can cause long-term damage to the psychological contract between employers and their employees, for example through applying pay increases or bonuses to senior executives when pay for other staff is frozen or when staff are being made redundant. Whether the damage is internal or external, the mismanagement of reward issues can impact on the ability of an organization to motivate, retain and recruit staff.

There is no way of avoiding risks in organizational life. Indeed, innovation is dependent on risk taking. Many decision makers use intuitive reasoning to consider options. This is not a bad starting point. However, organizations can take steps that enable them to identify significant risks and make considered judgements about how to deal with them. Risk management is about identifying, assessing and managing the uncertainties that impact on an organization's ability to achieve its aims and objectives. It is the basis for informed management. In this respect risk management is not just about dealing with what can go wrong, but exploring opportunities and identifying potential problems before they happen and making considered judgements. It is also about having contingency plans in place to deal with known but acceptable risks and in the last resort having a contingency plan to deal with the fall-out from events that do materialize.

The processes involved in organizational risk management are well defined and should be familiar to anyone who is an experienced project manager. Published standards include a British Standards Institute code of practice, standards published by the Association of Insurance and Risk Managers, ALARM and the Institute of Risk Management, and guidelines published by professional associations such as the accountancy bodies and by government ('the Orange Book'). Yet it is only recently that the importance of risk management in the reward function has been formally recognized. Indeed, only 17 per cent of respondents in a 2009 Chartered Institute of Personnel and Development (CIPD) survey felt that they were well prepared to handle risks relating to reward. Although a number of corporate governance codes have included guidance on board-level remuneration, it is only more recently that focus has turned towards organization-wide reward management risks. The need for this was highlighted in the UK Financial Services Authority (FSA) 2009 code of remuneration practice, which included as one of its six key principles that remuneration policies should be consistent with effective risk management. Although the code was published in direct response to the 2008–9 financial crisis and is focused on senior-level pay and incentives in the financial sector, many of the recommendations are capable of being adapted for other sectors. In 2009 the CIPD added to the guidance available by issuing a report and guidance on reward risk management.

This tool is not intended to replace the detailed guidance that is available from the CIPD or other sources. However, in describing the risk management process and a range of risk management tools, this tool aims to provide a basic guide to risk management for those who are involved in reward projects or have responsibility for managing reward policies or processes.

The risk management process

Any risk management process follows the same broad steps. These are:

- *Developing a framework for managing risk*: managing risk is easier if there is clarity about who is involved in risk management decisions, if there is a commonly held understanding about the level of risk that an organization is prepared to tolerate and if a process is set up to integrate risk management into established project and management processes. Risk identification is a subjective process, so it helps to get group input at a sufficient level of seniority to draw on colleagues' combined knowledge and experiences, and to have authority to take actions.
- *Risk identification*: the identification of significant risks.
- *Risk assessment*: categorizing the risks and then assessing the likelihood of those risks turning to reality and what impact they might have.

- *Risk control*: deciding how to treat the risks that have been identified.
- *Risk monitoring and review*: monitoring regularly, drawing on learnings and feeding this back into the process.

Developing a framework for managing risk

Figure 4.1 summarizes the questions that will help an organization to get started in developing a risk management framework and identifies issues relating to each question.

FIGURE 4.1 Developing a risk management framework

Question	Issues
What risk management protocols already exist in the organization? Is there a formal risk strategy? If there is an existing strategy, does it deal with any reward risks?	If there is an existing risk management system, could this be extended to deal with reward risks, or could the main features of the approach be adapted?
Is there clarity around the organization's appetite for risk? Is it clear what the tolerances are within your organization, or is there a need to start a dialogue about what these should be?	The answer to this question will depend on factors such as sectoral influences, leadership, culture, business model and the regulatory environment in which the organization operates.
Who can make meaningful contribution to discussions about reward risks? This may include: • senior management • HR function • internal audit • compliance • finance • legal.	The response should ensure that representation is at a sufficiently high level to confirm what level and type of reward risks the organization is prepared to tolerate.
Is it clear how risk monitoring can be brought into regular internal processes, and how often, eg as part of team or management meetings?	The answer to this question will help in deciding what reward management tools and processes are needed for ongoing monitoring and review.

Risk identification

In this initial stage risks are identified and categorized so that the most significant ones can be assessed in more detail. This requires having access to a range of useful intelligence. There are many sources of information that can help organizations to identify potential risks. Examples are listed in Figure 4.2.

FIGURE 4.2 Risk intelligence sources

Internal sources of information	External sources of information
• Organizational risk register • Management/staff meeting • Interviews • Questionnaires • Checklists using simple lists of questions based on experience/lessons learnt from previous projects or initiatives • Exit interviews • Equal pay audits • Employee attitude/engagement surveys • Reviews of policies and practices, including internal audit reports on existing approaches and reviews of proposed approaches • Business/management reports, such as management accounts, progress against strategy and objectives • HR management information, such as employee turnover, analyses of pay competitiveness, activity reports relating to grievances, disciplinary issues • Incidence of legal disputes with employees	• Supplier reports, eg from suppliers of outsourced services, including reports on compliance against agreed service levels • Industry benchmarking and research • Employment law briefings • Government consultation papers • Professional publications and briefings • Trend data relating to economic, demographic or social changes • Employer surveys

Risks can also be identified using standard analytical tools to review projects or processes, such as:

- SWOT analysis (strengths, weaknesses, opportunities, threats);
- PESTLE (political, economic, social, technical, legal, environmental factors).

Both of these tools involve breaking down elements of the project or process under a series of main headings in order to identify risk elements.

Risk assessment

The first stage of risk assessment involves categorizing the nature of risk that may occur. Most risk models involve grouping and assessing risks under a number of broad headings. These are described below.

Strategic risks relate to how closely activities are aligned with the organization's overall strategy. These risks may impact on the brand perception or internal misalignment of policies and procedures, and the realization of strategic reward risks may impact on the organization's ability to attract and retain staff.

Financial risks are about whether financial resources of the organization are being effectively managed. This is likely to be reflected in perceived value for money, financial viability or cost effectiveness.

Operational risks relate to the effectiveness of administrative or operational procedures or controls.

Legal and compliance risks relate to the nature of laws and regulations that an organization operates within.

Ethical risks are distinct from laws and regulations. Many reward issues that have hit the headlines have focused on the morality of reward interventions or actions. Even where rules allow certain activities, these may be at odds with a broader sense of right or wrong. Because remuneration systems are a dominant part of modern business and organizations, there is broad interest in the fairness of pay practices and the extent to which they indicate that the organization and people that work within them are acting with integrity. People expect organizations to do what is right and not just what is practical, feasible or profitable. Similarly, for employees a fair day's wage for a fair day's work isn't just about economic value but incorporates issues related to trust, work relationships and ethics. Reward systems are therefore powerful symbols of the values expressed by an organization and provide tangible evidence of how it enacts its moral standards and values.

Environmental risks relate to the physical environment. Although some organizations find this quite straightforward to assess, environmental issues are increasingly being brought into reward decisions, in the context of a stronger organizational focus on corporate and social responsibility. 'Cycle to work' schemes and company car schemes are two obvious reward mechanisms that can be linked to environmental issues.

The CIPD has included three additional reward-specific risk groups in addition to these risk groups in their guidance in response to their 2009 research on what reward practitioners had to say about say about reward risks:

- **Behavioural risks** relate to the potential misalignment between an organization's objectives and the behaviours that are encouraged by its reward practices. For example, an organization may state that it values teamwork but only incentivizes individual performance.

- **Implementation and change management risk**: this risk arises from how effectively an organization manages and implements change, potentially enhancing or reducing the impact of desired change. The two biggest risks identified by employers in the CIPD research fell into this area, namely poor reward communications and the inability to adapt reward policies and practices to the changing business environment (the latter is also an aspect of strategic risk).

- **Governance**: these are the risks relating to effective oversight of reward strategy. Effective governance sets the framework for managing strategic risk, particularly for senior executives.

FIGURE 4.3   Identifying risk groups

Nature of risk	Questions
Strategic	Is the reward system sufficiently aligned to organizational values and strategy?
	Does the reward system support the broader HR strategy and goals?
Financial	Is the reward system affordable under a range of different business scenarios? Are any aspects of the system particularly vulnerable in this regard?
	Are the costs of any insured benefits and pension arrangements being managed effectively?
	If any risks are self-insured, can the costs be fully met if any risk materializes?
	Are performance-related payments genuinely linked to improvements in performance and are payments funded from improved performance?
	Is the organization getting value for money from external vendors?
	Are the organization's taxation liabilities managed appropriately?
Behavioural	Does the organization communicate and reinforce the desired behaviours through its reward processes and policies?
	If relevant, are appropriate behaviours being rewarded through performance awards?
	Are levels of reward seen to be fair between employees?
Operational	Are personal data properly protected?
	Are appropriate checks made on any outsourced contracts to ensure that the provider is applying proper risk controls of their own?
	Are effective protections in place to minimize the potential for financial fraud?
	Does the reward/HR/payroll team have the required capability to manage reward processes?
	Do line managers have the necessary skills to play their part in managing reward processes?
Legal and compliance	Is the organization aware of potential liabilities under employment legislation?
	Are changes in legislation monitored as they occur?
	Has the organization kept track of and responded to any regulatory frameworks that apply to their sector?
	Is there an understanding of what exposure there may be to implied contractual terms?
Ethical	Does the organization's espoused principles relate to how reward is managed in practice?
	Does the organization have a clear sense of what is fair and what its ethical boundaries are relative to its interpretation of legal or regulatory requirements?
	Is management comfortable about explaining to others, internally and externally, the rationale for the organization's reward policies and practices?

FIGURE 4.3 *Continued*

Nature of risk	Questions
Governance	Has a remuneration committee or other body comprised of non-executive directors/trustees been set up to address senior-level remuneration?
	Does the committee have clear terms of reference?
	Is the remit of the remuneration/pay decision-making committee appropriately defined to ensure that decisions are made in the context of the organization's overall approach to people and reward management?
	Does the committee have sufficient knowledge of the organization, remuneration issues in general and organization-specific reward policies to make appropriate decisions?
Implementation/ change management	Are existing communications processes effective in supporting change?
	Do employees have a good understanding of the organization's reward arrangements?
	Is there internal management capability to deal with any changes to policy, procedure or practice?
	Does the organization have a culture of adaptability?
	Are relationships with staff representatives, unions and staff conducive to supporting change?

These groupings can be used to assess reward risks across the organization. Figure 4.3 lists key questions in respect of each risk group.

As a lot of the public debate about reward issues has focused on the morality of reward policies and practices, it may be appropriate to confirm whether more should be done to formalize organizational codes of behaviour, rather than relying on implicit norms and standards. The questions and issues highlighted in Figure 4.4 are based on an Institute of Business Ethics eight-point plan for developing a code of ethics. Although the questions are intended to cover all aspects of organizational behaviour, they apply equally well in reviewing reward management ethics.

After assessing the nature of the risks, the next step is to assess their potential impact. The most common approach is to develop and populate a grid that plots the probability of the risk occurring and the impact if it materializes. This is illustrated in Figure 4.5. The meanings of 'low', 'medium' and 'high' need to be agreed in order to complete the grid. The most important risks are those that score high/high for probability and impact.

Assessment against these two dimensions enables risks to be prioritized.

Controlling risk

When the most important risks have been identified, the organization needs to decide how to respond. Risk management guidance often refers to the four Ts of risk control; tolerate, treat, transfer, or terminate. Figure 4.6 lists

FIGURE 4.4   Developing a code of ethics

Question	Reward issues
Is the board/governing body committed to sound ethics?	The board/governing body needs to recognize that issues pertaining to reward are widely seen as ethical issues.
Is there an internal champion?	Unless a senior person such as the chief executive is prepared to drive the introduction of an ethics policy, the chances of it being a useful tool are not good.
Has the organization developed clear policies or a code of practice on ethics, including performance objectives?	A set of reward principles is likely to articulate the underlying principles that govern reward policies and practices. If this doesn't exist, consideration should be given to articulating what these are.
Has the board/senior management team assigned authority to senior management to implement its corporate ethics policy?	This is about assigning accountability to senior management for ensuring that its codes of ethics are not breached.
Is there clarity about what really bothers people internally?	Endorsing a standard code or set of principles from another organization will often not suffice. It is important to find out on what topics employees require guidance.
Does the framework address issues as they affect or are perceived by different constituents of the organization, such as shareholders, employees, customers, suppliers and local/national community?	Policies should be capable of being justified to all stakeholders.
Has the policy/code been issued widely and made known to the organization's stakeholders?	There is no point in having good practice if no one knows about it.
Is the policy/code integrated with other messages, for example though induction and training?	To be effective, the code/principles should be reinforced within broader employee communication and practices.

FIGURE 4.5   Likelihood and impact matrix

Nature of risk:			
Likelihood / Impact	Low	Medium	High
High			
Medium			
Low			

FIGURE 4.6   Risk control questions

Control approach	Questions to determine control response	Response
Tolerate, ie acknowledge and accept consequences	Can any part of the risk be accepted? Are the costs or implications of taking any action disproportionate to the potential benefit gained? (The answer to this question depends on the organization's appetite for risk.)	
Treat, ie mitigate the risk to reduce the probability of it occurring	What actions can be taken to constrain the risk to an acceptable level? If the risk cannot be reduced to an acceptable level, what contingency plans are needed to deal with events that cannot be controlled? The treatment of risks can be further subdivided into the following four categories: • Preventive: can controls be put in place to limit the likelihood of the risk occurring, for example by having appropriate governance controls? (This is the most common response to a risk.) • Corrective: this is what has to be done after the event, ie to recover against loss or damage, such as the payment of compensation, design of contract terms to allow recovery of overpayment or insurance to recover monies in case a risk is realized. • Directive: are controls in place to direct actions where critical risks have to be avoided, eg where people's safety or lives are at risk? • Detective: should appropriate controls be in place to monitor and assess what has happened (but without preventing it from happening in the first place)? These are only useful when the impact of the risk can be accepted, eg stock checking, post-project reviews.	
Transfer, ie deflect the risk to another party	If the organization is not competent or willing to manage the risk, can it be transferred to an external body, eg through insurance or outsourcing? (However, even if a risk is outsourced, the reputational risk usually stays with the organization, even if the nature of the risk changes. Also the organization needs to confirm that the outsourced operation is dealing with its own business risks appropriately. This can be done through requesting copies of risk management plans and assessment reports.)	
Terminate, ie eliminating potential cause	Can the risk be eliminated completely – and in doing so not create a different risk?	

a set of questions against each of these to enable an organization to assess which response is most appropriate.

Having plotted where each risk falls on the likelihood/impact matrix, and having addressed the questions about how to control the risk, an exercise can be undertaken to populate the matrix with a set of control responses. A partially completed example is provided in Figure 4.7.

FIGURE 4.7   Risk control responses

Likelihood / Impact	Low	Medium	High
High	Put contingency plan in place		Take immediate remedial action; contingency plan in place; review continuously
Medium		Tolerate: continue existing control measures; possible contingency plan	
Low	Example actions: tolerate: no action – continue control if required – review annually		Ensure preventative controls are in place

The final risk assessment step is to log each risk and record how it will be addressed. The risks are listed on one axis and the risk strategy is listed on the other. An example of a risk management register is shown in Figure 4.8. Keeping a register of risks enables them to be assessed regularly and updated when necessary.

FIGURE 4.8   Risk register

Risk	Controls	Residual risk (ie after controls have been applied)		Further actions	Owner of risk and review process
		Impact	**Likelihood**		

Risk monitoring and review

A risk analysis is not a one-off event. Instead risk management should be an integral part of decision making within the organization and any significant risks should be kept under regular review.

The tools and techniques described in this tool are most useful if risk management is regarded as an ongoing aspect of reward work. It is an integral part of effective project management and managing existing policies and procedures.

Even with effective risk management controls in place, it cannot be assumed that a worst-case scenario is so unrealistic that it won't happen. It may do, and if it does it is necessary to promptly develop and implement an emergency plan, identifying who has responsibility for taking the required actions. A key feature of the plan will be to manage the communications flow. This requires identifying the key stakeholders and considering what communication is needed for the following groups:

- employees;
- senior managers;
- shareholders or trustees;
- customers;
- public;
- relevant authorities;
- volunteers.

Key learnings

A number of key points emerge from risk management literature:

- There is no need to predict and eliminate every risk. An organization's risk management approach should be proportionate to the risks in the business and reflect their risk threshold.
- Establish a system for gathering reward risk intelligence.
- Don't reinvent the wheel. Use established risk management tools.
- Establish and maintain an appropriate level of risk awareness and review.

References

A risk management standard (2002) Association of Insurance and Risk Managers, ALARM and Institute of Risk Management, London

BS 31100 Code of practice for risk management (2008) British Standards Institute, London

Code of Remuneration Practice (2009) FSA, London

'Developing an effective code of ethics', Institute of Business Ethics website www.ibe.org.uk

Management of Risk – Principles and Concepts ('the Orange Book') (2004) HM Treasury, London

Managing reward risks: an integrated approach (2010) CIPD, London

Tool 05
Job evaluation

Introduction

Job evaluation is a systematic process for defining the relative worth or size of jobs within an organization in order to establish internal relativities. Decisions about what jobs are worth take place all the time. They may be made informally, based on assumptions about the value of a job in the marketplace or by comparison with other jobs in the organization. Or there may be a formal approach, either some type of job evaluation or 'levelling', or a systematic comparison with market rates.

Evaluating 'worth' leads directly or indirectly to decisions on where a job is placed in a level or grade within a hierarchy and therefore influences how much someone is paid. The performance of individuals also affects their pay – but this is not a matter for job evaluation, which is concerned with valuing the jobs people carry out, not how well they perform them.

Types of job evaluation

Analytical job evaluation

Analytical job evaluation is based on a methodology of breaking whole jobs down into a number of defined elements or factors such as responsibility, decisions and the knowledge and skill required. These are assumed to be present in all the jobs to be evaluated. Jobs are then compared factor by factor either with a graduated scale of points attached to a set of factors or with grade or role profiles analysed under the same factor headings. Analytical job evaluation can provide a defence in the UK against an equal pay claim.

The 2007 e-reward survey of job evaluation found that 70 per cent of respondents with formal job evaluation schemes used point-factor rating while 12 per cent used analytical matching. However, the latter is being increasingly used because it provides a quicker and less cumbersome but still analytical form of job evaluation. It is sometimes underpinned by a point-factor job evaluation scheme.

Non-analytical job evaluation

Non-analytical job evaluation involves comparing whole jobs, ie ones that are not analysed by reference to their elements or factors, in order to place them in a grade or a rank order. It does not provide a defence in an equal pay claim.

Levelling

Levelling is an approach to job evaluation that focuses on defining the levels of work in an organization and fitting jobs into those levels. The levels may be defined in terms of one factor such as decision making. It may serve as the basis for a pay structure but increasingly, levelling contributes to organizational analysis, provides guidance on career mapping and the development and description of international organization structures, and acts as a link to an information technology system such as PeopleSoft or SAP.

Market pricing

Market pricing is the process of obtaining information on market rates (market rate analysis) to inform decisions on pay structures and individual rates of pay.

Purpose and contents of the tool

The tool deals with the steps required to develop the most popular form of job evaluation, ie point-factor rating. However, it does refer to the design of analytical matching schemes which can function independently but are often associated with a point-factor scheme. A typical method is to design and test a point-factor scheme and then use the factors included in that scheme as the basis for analytical matching. This is the approach used in this tool. The tool is set out under the following headings:

- The review and development sequence;
- Step 1: Analyse present arrangements;
- Step 2: Decide approach to job evaluation in principle;
- Step 3: Select and brief project team;
- Step 4: Formulate communications strategy;
- Step 5: Decide on features of new scheme;
- Step 6: Prepare project programme;
- Step 7: Develop basic factor plan;
- Step 8: Select and analyse test jobs;

- Step 9: Test basic factor plan;
- Step 10: Amend basic factor plan as necessary;
- Step 11: Decide on weighting;
- Step 12: Confirm final factor plan;
- Step 13: Computerize;
- Step 14: Apply scheme to benchmark jobs;
- Step 15: Conduct market rate analysis;
- Step 16: Design grade and pay structure;
- Step 17: Develop analytical matching scheme;
- Step 18: Implement.

See Figure 5.1.

FIGURE 5.1   The job evaluation review and development
sequence

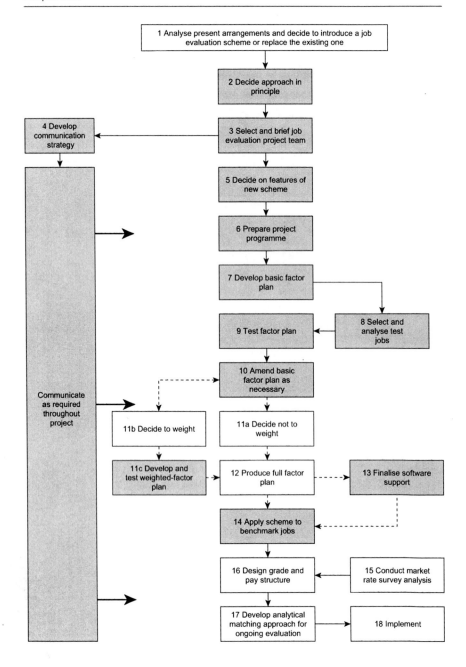

Step 1: Analyse present job evaluation arrangements

A preliminary assessment should be made of whether or not the present arrangements for job evaluation should be replaced or whether to introduce formal job evaluation. It is desirable to involve stakeholders – senior management, line managers, staff and staff representatives – in this assessment. Figure 5.2 can be used where there is an existing job evaluation scheme. Use can also be made of surveys, special workshops or focus groups, or a consultative forum. The aim should be to reach agreement on whether or not to go ahead and replace an existing scheme or introduce one for the first time.

FIGURE 5.2   Analysis of current job evaluation scheme

	Statement	Fully agree	Partly agree	Partly disagree	Fully disagree
1	The present arrangements for valuing and grading jobs are quite satisfactory.				
2	Our scheme ensures that there are no grading problems.				
3	The factors in our scheme are no longer appropriate.				
4	Our scheme has decayed.				
5	Our scheme prevents grade drift.				
6	Our scheme would provide a good defence in an equal pay case.				
7	The weightings of factors in the scheme are inappropriate.				
8	There is no gender bias in the scheme's factors and weightings.				
9	The scheme is bureaucratic, paper intensive and time wasting.				
10	People generally understand how the scheme works.				

Step 2: Decide approach to job evaluation in principle

When the present arrangements have been analysed, a decision can be made in principle on the approach to job evaluation. This will provide the basis for a brief to a design project team. The choices are set out in Figure 5.3. The only schemes mentioned are analytical on the grounds that non-analytical approaches are inappropriate because it can be difficult to fit complex jobs into a grade without using over-elaborate grade definitions; the definitions tend to be so generalized that they are not much help in evaluating borderline cases or making comparisons between individual jobs and importantly, they do not provide a defence in an equal value case.

The rest of this tool assumes that the choice has been made to introduce a combined tailor-made scheme which may or may not be computer aided.

FIGURE 5.3 Choice of approach

Choice	Factors to be taken into account	Decision
Make no change	• Extent to which present arrangements are satisfactory • Need to avoid disruption • Cost considerations	
Introduce new point-factor scheme or substantially amend existing one	• Advantages – analytical, provide equal pay claim defence • Disadvantages – time consuming, bureaucratic • The fact that this is by far the most popular approach	
Introduce analytical matching	• Advantages – analytical, much less time consuming than point-factor rating • Disadvantages – may not resolve equity problems, not a guaranteed defence in an equal pay case, may need to be underpinned by point-factor evaluation	
Introduce combined scheme, ie an underpinning point-factor scheme used to develop grade structure and as backup, and an analytical matching scheme for ongoing evaluations	• Provides support to analytical matching • Reduces time for ongoing evaluations • Provides defence in equal pay case • Can be complex and difficult to understand	
Purchase 'ready-made' scheme from consultant	• Scheme well established • Consultants experienced in implementation • Linked to market rate database • May not fit culture and circumstances of organization • Could be expensive	

FIGURE 5.3 *Continued*

Choice	Factors to be taken into account	Decision
Develop own 'tailor-made' scheme	• Scheme should fit • Those involved in development should 'own' scheme • But, untried and could be time consuming and expensive to develop in terms of the human resources required	
Consider using a computer-aided approach	• The development of a computer-aided approach usually takes place after the factor plan has been finalized and a paper scheme (ie one that has not been computerized) has been produced. • A final decision is not required at this stage although it may be agreed that one of the proprietary brands should be tested when the paper scheme is ready.	

Step 3: Select and brief project team

It is highly desirable to set up a project team to oversee and take part in the project. The composition of the design team and how they should be briefed could have been determined at Step 1. It should reflect the diversity of the organization. Facilitation and technical support can be provided by HR, possibly with the help of outside consultants. The support will include the detailed work of job analysis and developing and testing factor plans.

The terms of reference for the project team could be to:

- agree the overall approach to job evaluation;
- develop and assist in the implementation of a communications strategy;
- provide ideas and input at all stages of the scheme design, for example drawing up the factor plan;
- function as a sounding board for the detailed design work that takes place outside the project team meetings;
- take part in tests of the proposed scheme;

- review the outcome of tests and progress generally;
- act as an advocate for the project;
- help with communicating information about the project to employees.

Once the design work has been completed, the project team or a selection of its members could form a job evaluation panel to conduct further evaluations of benchmark and other jobs.

Step 4: Develop communications strategy

Job evaluation schemes can arouse intense suspicion. It is therefore essential to have a strategy for communicating information about the scheme. The strategy may be developed in consultation with the project team and should cover what should be communicated, who it should be communicated to and how it should be communicated. Checklists of the major points which might be included in the communications strategy are set out in Figure 5.4.

FIGURE 5.4   Communications strategy

Strategy area	Strategy contents
What	• The purpose of the exercise • The evaluation process • The outcomes, eg a new grade and pay structure • The fact that job evaluation is not concerned with individual performance • An undertaking that no one's pay will decrease when the new pay structure is increased but that no one should expect to get an increase • Assimilation and protection arrangements • (It is best not to commit to a definite completion date – it often takes longer than you think.)
Who	• Top management • Line managers • Staff • Trade unions
How	• Overall oral briefings by management • Team briefings • Written communications • The intranet • Special bulletins (attach to payslips) • Informal question-and-answer sessions or 'town hall' meetings • Set up a network of 'champions' (not from HR) who can spread information about the project.

Step 5: Decide on features of new scheme

At this stage the project team should consider very broadly the design options available as a framework for the more detailed development programme. The options are listed in Figure 5.5. The decisions made now are interim and could be amended later.

FIGURE 5.5   Choice of features

Design area	Options	Interim decision
Job evaluation factors	There will be a choice on the number and types of factors. The number of factors can vary widely.	
Factor levels	There will be choice on the number of levels and whether or not there should be the same number of levels in each factor. Typically, there are five or six levels.	
Scoring progression	Scoring intervals between levels can be either arithmetic or geometrical.	
Weighting	Schemes can be unweighted, or if they are weighted, this can be explicit or implicit.	

At this stage a view should also be reached on the characteristics of the scheme. These can be expressed as design principles that can be used to review the design to ensure that the scheme will effectively assess relative values and avoid discrimination or bias. A checklist is given in Figure 5.6.

FIGURE 5.6   Checklist of design principles

- The scheme should be based on a thorough analysis of the jobs to be covered and the types of demands made on those jobs to determine what factors are appropriate.
- The scheme should facilitate impartial judgements of relative job size.
- The factors used in the scheme should cover the whole range of jobs to be evaluated at all levels without favouring any particular type of job or occupation and without discriminating on the grounds of gender, race, disability, age or for any other reason – the scheme should fairly measure features of female-dominated jobs as well as male-dominated jobs.
- Through the use of common factors and methods of analysis and evaluation, the scheme should enable benchmarking to take place of the relativities between jobs in different functions or job families.
- The factors should be clearly defined and differentiated – there should be no double counting.
- The levels should be defined and graduated carefully.
- Gender bias must be avoided in the choice of factors, the wording of factor and level definitions and the factor weightings – checks should be carried out to identify any bias.

Step 6: Prepare project programme

A project programme should be prepared in as much detail as possible. This will provide the basis for managing the project. A programme for a large, complex organization set out as a bar chart is illustrated in Figure 5.7.

FIGURE 5.7   Project plan bar chart

Activities	Months
	1 2 3 4 5 6 7 8 9 10 11 12 13 14 15 16 17 18 19 20 21 22 23 24
1 Agree deliverables	▬
1 Design and test scheme	▬▬▬▬▬▬▬▬▬▬
2 Evaluate benchmark jobs	▬▬▬▬
3 Design grade structure	▬
4 Evaluate remaining jobs	▬▬▬▬
5 Conduct market survey	▬▬▬▬
6 Design the pay structure	▬
7 Implement	▬

Step 7: Develop basic factor plan

A factor plan is the key component in a point-factor job evaluation. Its purpose is to provide an analytical framework that will guide evaluators in making decisions on the relative value of jobs. The main features are as follows:

- The plan takes the form of a matrix consisting of a number of factors (a factor is a criterion for judging the value of a job in one particular aspect or characteristic of the work involved), which are divided into a number of levels that can be used to determine the extent to which the factor is present in a job.
- Each of these levels has a points score attached to it so that when a decision is made on the level at which a factor is present in a job a score can be attached to it.
- The scores for each factor are then added to produce a total score.

- A plan may be unweighted, ie each factor has the same maximum number of points (the sum of the points attached to each level).
- Alternatively, it may be either implicitly weighted – ie one or more factors have a greater range of points attached to them at this stage because some factors have more levels than the rest – or explicitly weighted if any factors have additional points allocated to them even though they have the same number of levels.

At this stage the basic plan is not weighted. A decision whether or not to have weighting is made after the basic plan has been tested.

The process of developing a basic factor plan is described below.

Identify and define factors

Guidelines for selecting factors and avoiding gender bias are given in Figure 5.8.

FIGURE 5.8   Guidelines for selecting factors

- The factors must be capable of identifying relevant and important differences between jobs that will support the creation of a rank order of the jobs to be covered by the scheme.
- The factors should between them measure all significant job features and should be of broadly comparable scope.
- The factors should reflect the values of the organization.
- They should apply equally well to different types of work including specialists and generalists, lower-level and higher-level jobs, and not be biased in favour of one gender or group.
- The whole range of jobs to be evaluated at all levels should be covered without favouring men or women, people belonging to a particular racial group, different age groups or any particular job or occupation.
- The scheme should fairly measure features of female-dominated jobs as well as male-dominated jobs.
- The choice should not lead to discrimination on the grounds of gender, race, disability, religion, age or for any other reason. Experience should not be included as a factor because it could be discriminatory either on the grounds of gender or age. The same principle applies to education or qualifications as stand-alone factors.
- Job features frequently found in jobs carried out mainly by one gender should not be omitted, for example manual dexterity, interpersonal skills and 'caring' responsibilities. However, if such features are included, it is important that the scheme captures the range of skills across all jobs, including those that might be dominated by another gender.
- Double counting should be avoided, ie each factor must be independent of every other factor – the more factors (or sub-factors) in the plan, the higher the probability that double counting will take place.
- Elision or compression of more than one significant job feature under a single factor heading should be avoided. If important factors are compressed with others, it means that they could be undervalued.
- The factor definitions should be clear, relevant and understandable and written in a way that is meaningful to those who will use the scheme.
- The factors should be acceptable to those who will be covered by the scheme.

Examples of factor definitions are given in Figure 5.9.

FIGURE 5.9 Examples of factor definitions

Factor	Definition
1 Knowledge and skills	The levels of professional, specialist, technical, administrative or operational knowledge and skills required to carry out the role effectively
2 Contribution	The contribution made to achieving the objectives of the team, department or organization
3 Communicating	The requirement to communicate orally and in writing to individuals and groups of people inside and outside the organization and to external bodies
4 Interpersonal skills	The level of skill required to work well with others, to exercise leadership, to respond to people's requests, to handle difficult cases, to argue a case, to negotiate and to exert influence
5 Planning and organizing	The requirement to plan, schedule and coordinate work, to allocate priorities and to meet deadlines
6 Judgement and decision making	The requirement to exercise judgement in making decisions and solving problems, including the degree to which the work involves choice of action and/or creativity
7 Freedom to act	The degree to which independent action has to be taken, bearing in mind the level of control or guidance provided and the extent to which the work is supervised
8 Complexity	The variety and diversity of the work carried out, the decisions to be made and the knowledge and skills used
9 Responsibility for resources	The size of the resources controlled in terms of people, money, equipment, facilities etc
10 Demands on the role holder	The demands made by the role on the role holder because of work pressures (including those arising from handling emotional situations), non-social hours or a considerable amount of travelling

Define factor levels

There are typically five or six levels. It is usual to have the same number of levels for each factor although more levels may be assigned to one or two factors. In which case, the plan is said to be implicitly weighted because more points are available in the factors with extra levels. Guidelines on defining levels are given in Figure 5.10.

FIGURE 5.10   Guidelines for defining factor levels

- Consider the number of levels (often four, five, six or seven) which may be needed to reflect the range of responsibilities and demands in the jobs covered by the scheme. Analyse what would characterize the highest or lowest level for each factor and how these should be described.
- Decide provisionally on the number of levels (say three) between the highest and lowest level so that the level structure reflects the graduation in responsibilities or demands. (This decision could be amended following the process of defining levels, which might reveal that more or fewer levels are required.)
- Define each level as clearly as possible to help evaluators make 'best-fit' decisions when they compare role data with level definitions.
- Ensure that the levels cover the whole range of demands in this factor that are likely to arise in the jobs with which the evaluation scheme is concerned.
- Relate the content of level definitions to the definition of the factor concerned and ensure that it does not overlap with other factors.
- Ensure that the factor levels represent clear and recognizable steps in demand.
- Provide for uniform progression in the definitions, level by level from the lowest to the highest. There should be no gaps or undefined intermediate levels that might lead to evaluators finding it difficult to be confident about the allocation of a level of demand.
- Define levels in absolute, not relative, terms. So far as possible any dimensions should be defined. They should not rely upon a succession of undefined comparatives, eg small, medium, large.
- Ensure that each level definition stands on its own. Level definitions should not be defined by reference to a lower or higher level, ie it is insufficient to define a level in words to the effect that it is a higher (or lower) version of an adjacent level.

Develop scoring model

The next step is to decide on the scoring model. Each level in the factor plan has to be allocated a points value so that there is a scoring progression from the lowest to the highest level. A decision needs to be made on how to set the scoring progression within each factor.

There are two methods. First, the arithmetic or linear approach assumes that there are consistent step differences between factor levels – eg a five-level factor might be scored 10, 20, 30, 40 and 50. Alternatively, geometric scoring assumes that there are larger score differences at each successive level in the hierarchy to reflect progressive increases in responsibility. Thus the levels may be scored 10, 20, 35, 55 and 80, rather than 10, 20, 30, 40 and 50. This increases the scoring differentiation between higher-level jobs.

Step 8: Select and analyse test jobs

The basic scored but not explicitly weighted factor plan needs to be tested on a representative sample of jobs (sometimes called benchmark jobs,

FIGURE 5.11   Selection of test jobs matrix

	Function A	*Function B*	*Function C*	*Function D*	*Function E*
Level 1					
Level 2					
Level 3					
Level 4					
Level 5					

FIGURE 5.12   Format for job analysis/description

Job title		
Responsible to		
Responsible to job holder		
Overall purpose of job		
Key result areas		
Factor analysis	Factor 1	
	Factor 2	
	Factor 3	
	Factor 4	
	Factor 5	
	Factor 6	

although the term test jobs is more accurate). The sample should include jobs from each of the main levels in the major functions. The choice could take account of the levels in the basic factor plan although at this stage this would only be a provisional assumption for test purposes. A matrix as illustrated in Figure 5.11 can be used in making the choice.

The jobs from which the selection is made will need to be identified and the sample is unlikely to be less than 20 per cent of the distinct jobs in the organization – and in complex situations could be much more. The number should be sufficient to provide a good basis for testing the draft factor plan by assessing the extent to which it has produced an acceptable rank order for the test jobs.

The analysis should cover the overall purpose and key activities of the job and include a brief description of the requirements or demands of the job under each of the factor headings. Sufficient detail should be included to enable a job evaluation panel to match a job's characteristics for a factor with the most appropriate level in that factor. A standard format for the job analysis and the derived job description can be used as illustrated in Figure 5.12.

A questionnaire as illustrated in Figure 5.13 can be used to gather the information.

FIGURE 5.13   Job analysis questionnaire

What is the overall purpose of your job?	
What are the main activities for which you are responsible? (Most jobs can be described in a relatively small number of key headings.)	
Knowledge and skills required What are the basic skills required to do your job? Are any specific professional, technical or vocational skills or qualifications required to do the job? On what kind of things do other people come to you for information, advice or as a source of expertise?	
Interpersonal skills Who do you have dealings with on a regular basis? What is the nature of these relationships, eg giving information, providing professional or technical advice, influencing or persuading people, exercising leadership? Give examples.	

FIGURE 5.13 *Continued*

What is the overall purpose of your job?	
Planning and organizing Give examples of what you have to plan for/prioritize in your work either for yourself or others. Do you have to organize the work of others? If so, give examples.	
Judgement and decision making Give examples of the actions and decisions you are free to make without needing guidance or approval from anyone else. Describe how regularly and on what activities your work requires supervision. Describe the extent to which your work is guided by procedures or precedents. Does your job require you to develop new ideas, products, services or practices or to find new ways of working? Give examples.	
Complexity What is the range or variety of tasks you have to carry out or decisions you have to make? Give examples. How often do you find that you have to do something entirely different?	
Responsibility for resources How many people, if any, do you manage directly? For how many people, if any, have you overall responsibility? For what equipment or facilities are you responsible? Do you control a financial budget? If so, how much?	

Step 9: Test basic factor plan

Aim

The aim of this initial test is to check on the extent to which:

- the factors are appropriate;
- level definitions are worded clearly and graduated properly;

- level definitions provide good guidance on the allocation of factor levels to evaluators and thus enable consistent evaluations to be made;
- as far as can be judged, the evaluation produces a valid result.

The test can also begin the process of establishing conventions that are formed as evaluators gain experience in using the factor plan. They provide guidance on how level definitions and the information about a job can be interpreted in making a 'matching' decision on the factor level to be allocated.

Another important purpose of the test is to provide evaluators with experience and training in the process of evaluation. If a project team is used, which is normal practice, this test may be the first time its members have been involved in job evaluation. Facilitators of project teams have the important role of providing guidance and training to team members. They should themselves have experience of job evaluation and if that experience is not available within the organization there is a strong case for getting outside help.

Conducting evaluations

There is a choice of approach in carrying out test evaluations. Either the panel evaluates all jobs together, or jobs are evaluated by an analyst or subgroup of evaluators (pairs or more), and the full panel are then used to review the initial evaluations. There are three methods of evaluation from which a choice can be made:

- Factor by factor. The panel takes each factor in turn and evaluates all jobs in respect of that factor, ie whole jobs are not evaluated in turn. This is the best method.
- Whole jobs disclosed. Each panel member evaluates whole jobs factor by factor and then informs the panel of their conclusions.
- Whole jobs undisclosed. This is a variation of the second approach where the whole panel is involved in evaluating each job. Each panel member evaluates whole jobs factor by factor but does not communicate their views formally to other members of the panel. Instead, the panel as a whole discusses and agrees the evaluation of each factor in turn to produce a total job evaluation score.

Assessing the test outcome

An assessment should be made of the extent to which the factor plan (choice of factors, number of levels and level definitions) is appropriate and provides the guidance required, and of the extent to which the information provided about the jobs was adequate. In the former case, it will be necessary to revise the factor plan (Step 10). In the latter case it will be necessary to obtain additional data about the jobs by revising the job description or calling for specific information from job holders or their managers.

In addition, an overall ranking test can be conducted. This involves first placing the test jobs in rank order according to their scores (this is why an adequate number of test jobs is required). The project team then considers the extent to which it is believed the rank order is valid in the sense that the evaluations correctly indicate relative job value. There is no single, simple test that will establish the validity of a factor plan. The methods available are as follows:

- Reference ranking. The team compares the ranking produced by the job evaluation with the rank order produced by a ranking exercise. The technique of paired comparison may be used to guide the ranking process.

- Hierarchy comparisons. The rank order produced by the test is compared with the existing organizational hierarchy and any obvious discrepancies are investigated. However, care must be taken not to assume that the existing hierarchy is the correct one.

- External market test. Compare the internal rank order with that existing in comparable jobs elsewhere. But this may reflect pay differentials between job families, rather than internal measures of job worth. It may also replicate existing inequities between male and female jobs.

- The 'felt fair test'. The rank order produced by the test is compared with what the job evaluation panel 'feels' is the fair and therefore appropriate ranking, and discrepancies are identified. This is dangerous because it is liable simply to reproduce existing prejudices.

A common practice is to start with reference ranking and use one or more of the other methods to check on the ranking outcome.

If the rankings produced by job evaluation are not acceptable, it is necessary to establish why. There are three basic possible reasons:

- Inadequacies in the factor plan in terms of the choice of factors, the number of levels, the definition of levels or the scoring system, in which case it will need to be amended (Step 10).

- Misjudgements by the panel, in which case consideration will need to be given to revisiting evaluations, especially if only a few jobs stick out like a sore thumb as being wrongly evaluated (this process is called 'sore-thumbing').

- The possibility that some factors are more important than others and have not been given sufficient weight, in which case a decision may be made to provide for explicit weighting (Step 11).

Step 10: Amend basic factor plan as necessary

The initial test will almost certainly reveal the need to amend factor level definitions and it may indicate that more radical changes to the factor plan are required, for example in the choice of factors or the number of levels. Following any amendments it is desirable to retest the basic plan. This is time consuming, which is why a job evaluation exercise can be a lengthy process. But this is the time to get it right.

Step 11: Decide on weighting

Weighting recognizes that there are differences in the importance of factors by allocating more or fewer points to them. The choice is first between weighting or not weighting factors.

If weighting is considered desirable, possibly on the basis of the initial test of the basic factor plan, there is a choice between explicit and implicit weighting.

Explicit weighting means increasing the maximum points available for what were regarded as more important factors.

Implicit weighting means allocating more levels and therefore points to some factors rather than others. Implicit weighting is most likely to take place when there are a large number of factors – 10 or more – and the impact of explicitly weighting any factors is less (unless the weighting is so disproportionate that the non-weighted factors become immaterial). Implicit weighting can have taken place when the basic factor plan was produced and the test will need to review if this was appropriate. Alternatively, it may be decided that some factors do need additional levels, in which case the plan will have been implicitly weighted.

Weighting may be considered desirable by some people but there is no reliable scientific method of deciding where it should take place and how much it should be.

One pseudo-scientific approach is multiple linear regression analysis which is used to predict the combination of weights that will replicate a reference ranking. But apart from being complex, this may simply reproduce an existing rank order (and perpetuate gender discrimination) and thus risk subverting the purpose of job evaluation, which is to re-examine relative values rather than accept the status quo.

The most common but highly judgemental approach is for the project team to discuss and agree subjective views on which factors are more impor-tant and allocate additional points or extra levels accordingly. Another method of deciding on explicit weighting, ie extra points, is to get each member of the team to distribute 100 points among the factors. The results are then revealed to the whole team, which reaches an agreement on the most acceptable distribution. This discussion may be expected to take account of guiding principles such as that no factor will have a weighting of less than 5 per cent or more than 30 per cent.

The weighted plan should be retested on the test jobs to ensure that it produces valid results.

Step 12: Produce full factor plan

The basic factor plan (the range of factors and level definitions) produced after the initial test will be finalized, taking into account decisions on weighting.

It is also necessary at this stage to draw up guidelines as set out in Figure 5.14 on the operation of the scheme, which will be particularly concerned with the steps needed to avoid gender bias. Steps should also be taken to set up a permanent job evaluation panel to manage and monitor the scheme.

FIGURE 5.14 Guidelines for operating a job evaluation scheme

- The scheme should be transparent; everyone concerned should know how it works – the basis upon which the evaluations are produced.
- Appropriate proportions of women, ethnic minorities and people with disabilities should be involved in the process of applying job evaluation.
- The quality of role analysis should be monitored to ensure that analyses produce accurate and relevant information that will inform the job evaluation process and will not be biased.
- Consistency checks should be built into operating procedures.
- The outcomes of evaluations should be examined to ensure that gender or any other form of bias has not occurred.
- Particular care is necessary to ensure that the outcomes of job evaluation do not simply replicate the existing hierarchy – it is to be expected that a job evaluation exercise will challenge present relativities.
- All those involved in role analysis and job evaluation should be thoroughly trained in the operation of the scheme and in how to avoid bias.
- Special care should be taken in developing a grade structure following a job evaluation exercise to ensure that grade boundaries are placed appropriately and that the allocation of jobs to grades is not in itself discriminatory.
- There should be scope for the review of evaluations and for appeals against gradings.
- The scheme should be monitored to ensure that it is being operated properly and that it is still fit for its purpose.

Step 13: Consider software support

Consideration at this stage can be given to the possibility of introducing computer-aided evaluation. The two types are:

- Using software to apply predetermined rules to convert the data into scores for each factor and produce a total score. This is the most common approach.

- Interactive computer-aided schemes in which the job holder and their manager sit in front of a PC and are presented with a series of logically interrelated questions, the answers to which lead to a score for each of the built-in factors in turn and a total score.

The advantages and disadvantages of computer-aided evaluation are set out in Figure 5.15.

FIGURE 5.15 Advantages and disadvantages of computer-aided job evaluation

Advantages	Disadvantages
• Greater consistency may be achieved – the same input information gives the same output result. • The speed of evaluations can be increased. • Facilities are provided for sorting, analysing, reporting on the input information and system outputs and for record keeping on a database. • The resources required are reduced.	• May be expensive. • May be elaborate or have the feel of a 'black box'. • May lack transparency. • Means abandoning the involvement of employees and their representatives in the traditional panel approach.

A computer-aided system is usually based on the paper-based system's factor plan. So it needs to be tested on the same jobs used for testing the paper-based system to ensure that it replicates the paper scheme's results.

Step 14: Apply scheme to benchmark jobs

The final paper or computer-aided scheme is used to evaluate benchmark jobs (except in a small organization where all jobs may be evaluated). These are typical jobs that represent the different occupations and levels of work in an organization and are used as points of reference with which other jobs can be compared and evaluated. The evaluated benchmark jobs provide the basis for designing a grade structure and are used in analytical matching as described below (Step 17). They will include the test jobs but it may be necessary to select additional ones to provide a sufficient number for designing a grade structure.

Step 15: Conduct market rate analysis

An analysis of market rates is usually required to provide the information needed to develop a pay structure. The actions required to conduct the analysis are described in the market rate analysis tool (Tool 6).

Step 16: Design grade and pay structure

The benchmark jobs are ranked according to their scores and divided into grades. Tool 7, on base pay management, provides detailed guidance.

Step 17: Develop analytical matching approach

Analytical matching involves matching jobs to be evaluated on a factor-by-factor basis either with analytical grade definitions (grade profiles) or analytical job descriptions for benchmark posts (role profiles). The development sequence is illustrated in Figure 5.16.

FIGURE 5.16 Analytical matching job evaluation scheme development sequence

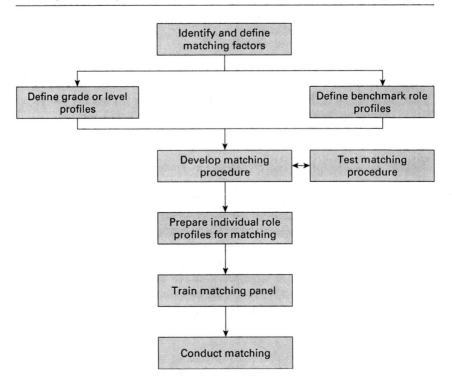

Where analytical matching is developed to support a point factor scheme, the first two steps will involve looking at the pattern of evaluation results for each grade and developing grade/level profiles that reflect the typical pattern of results, factor by factor.

Matching procedure

The matching procedure may be defined as a formal protocol that specifies:

- what constitutes a perfect match, ie where all the elements in the role profile match all the elements in the grade or benchmark role profile;
- the number of matches required of individual elements to indicate that a profile match is justified, for example six out of 10; but it is usual to restrict the mismatches allowed to fairly small variations – if there are any large ones, the match would be invalidated;
- any elements that must match for there to be a profile match; for example, it may be decided that there must be a match for an element covering knowledge and skills;
- the procedure for grading if there has been a mismatch; this may specify a full evaluation of the role if the matching process is underpinned by a point-factor or proprietary analytical scheme.

Step 18: Implement

Implementation involves assimilating employees to the new grade and pay structure, providing for pay protection, communicating the results to employees and hearing appeals in accordance with an appeals procedure.

Assimilation

A policy is required on how employees should be assimilated into a new pay structure resulting from job evaluation. This is described in Tool 7 on base pay management.

Communicating results

Details should be communicated to all employees of the new grade and pay structure, how jobs are graded within the structure and how pay progression takes place within grades.

Individual employees should be told the grade of their job, their rate of pay and the scope for pay progression. If their pay is below the minimum of the grade ('green-circled'), they should be informed of the arrangements for bringing their pay up to the minimum for their new grade. If their pay is above the maximum of the grade ('red-circled') they should be told how their pay will be protected.

Appeals

It is necessary to have a published procedure for hearing appeals. The procedure should set out:

- the grounds upon which an appeal can be made, eg that an individual believes that they have been under-graded;
- the body that should hear the appeal, often a specially constituted appeals panel whose members should not have been involved in the original evaluation;
- the procedure for hearing the appeal, for example obtaining supporting evidence from the appellant, requesting a rationale from the original evaluation panel for their decision, requesting a re-evaluation by the original panel (or by a specially formed panel).

References

Armstrong, M and Cummins, A (2008) *Valuing Roles*, Kogan Page, London
e-reward Survey of Job Evaluation (2007), e-reward, Stockport

Tool 06
Market analysis

Introduction

Market analysis is the process of researching and analysing external market pay and benefits data. The result of the process is information that can be used to benchmark the competitiveness of an organization's remuneration levels, policies and practices. There are many reasons for doing this. These include creating or validating a grade structure or set of pay ranges, checking out the external market before recruiting into a new position, developing a new bonus scheme or responding to recruitment or retention problems. Whatever the reason, it is necessary to find good data, understand whether the data are reliable, and turn raw data into meaningful analyses that can be used internally.

No magic wand can be waved to create the 'answer' when it comes to providing accurate market data. Indeed, in agreeing that a market analysis is required, expectations need to be set with line management. All too many managers and senior executives – and, indeed, employees – believe that it is not only possible, but relatively simple, to establish a 'correct' rate for any given job, in any industry, in any location, for any age or experience level – preferably to the nearest pound. However, in practice, there is no such thing as wholly objective data or a 'right' answer. Even the most thorough survey is reliant on the quality of data available and the mix of survey participants. Ultimately judgement has to be applied in interpreting the market analysis.

This tool describes the steps required to analyse external remuneration data.

The market analysis process

The market analysis process consists of the following six steps:

- Preparation: confirming the need for market analysis and who will do it;
- Choosing jobs for external comparison: this involves being realistic about the extent to which it is possible to obtain a reasonable comparison externally;
- Defining data collection criteria;
- Matching the organization's jobs to the external market;
- Analysing and interpreting data: how to make use of the raw data that have been gathered;
- Presenting the results to internal audiences.

Step 1: Preparation

Before embarking on a market analysis exercise, it is necessary to make sure that the problem is genuinely pay related. Sometimes issues that are reportedly related to pay disguise a range of non-pay-related matters. Figure 6.1 provides a checklist of issues that sometimes arise as a market analysis request but which should be reviewed before confirming that a market analysis is appropriate.

It is important to exhaust other options before deciding that the appropriate solution is pay related. As pay is the most tangible and visible element of the total reward package, there could well be greater long-term implications and risk in applying a pay solution than resolving the issue through other means.

If there is a need to analyse external market data, the next question is who will do it. The analysis can be done internally or outsourced to a third-party provider. The choice of whether to conduct the analysis in-house or externally depends on:

- whether the organization has good access to relevant data through salary surveys or whether there is a need to buy access to data;
- availability and competence of internal expertise;
- cost of external expertise;
- perceived validity of results.

A summary of what to consider in deciding whether to conduct market analysis internally or to commission a third party to do the work is provided in Figure 6.2.

FIGURE 6.1 Checklist: alternatives to market analysis

Issue	Questions
Retention problem	Are there broader issues relating to management style or working practices?
	If an individual is threatening to leave for salary reasons, has proper consideration been given to whether the organization should respond with salary, whether further development opportunities could be offered, or indeed whether the individual is so indispensable that something should be done to prevent them leaving?
Recruitment difficulties	Has the recruitment effort been targeted effectively?
	Has there been a clear recruitment strategy, including appropriate advertising?
	Have alternative recruitment methods been considered, eg journals, web campaign, agencies?
	Would alternative/flexible working patterns make it easier to recruit, eg job share, part-time working, home working?
	Has consideration been given to developing the skills required in-house as an alternative to recruiting externally?
External market intelligence indicating high salaries	To what extent is this external market information really causing a problem? Before taking any action consider these questions:
	• Is the external information from a valid source, ie salary surveys rather than isolated recruitment advertisements?
	• Is there evidence that a recruitment agency is seeking to 'talk up' the market?
	• Does the information fully compare all aspects of the remuneration package?
	• Is this information actually causing difficulties in recruitment or retention?

FIGURE 6.2   Checklist: Choosing the market analysis approach

Checklist	Yes/no; comments
Do you already have access to good-quality data through survey participation/other sources?	
If data aren't readily available, can they be purchased from a third-party provider, or is there a need to research other companies directly? If so, would the companies concerned be more likely to respond directly to the company or through a third-party provider?	
Do you want to build a body of knowledge internally about the external market in order to be able to discuss market data issues confidently with line management, HR colleagues or remuneration committee?	
Do you want to develop an understanding of how robust the external market data are and develop the appropriate skills to interpret data consistently?	
Is there internal capability and time to deal with external data queries internally – or is it easier to pay for this? If the latter, is a budget available for this? (Third-party analysis is relatively expensive compared with buying a salary survey.)	
If data analysis is conducted internally, will analysis have credibility with management, or is there a perceived need for external validation?	
If your organization has a market-based pay system, is there sufficient internal knowledge of the pay data and their sources to be able to explain and justify the data to an employment tribunal if required? (It would be the organization's responsibility to do this, not the third-party provider.)	

Step 2: Choosing jobs for external comparison

Whether the analysis is conducted internally or externally, it will be more credible if it can be demonstrated that a systematic process has been used. Having decided that a market assessment is required, the next step is to decide which jobs need to be included. For one-off jobs this may look straightforward. However, it may be necessary to consider whether there are potentially any implications for other jobs. For example, does the job fall into a hierarchy of similar roles where the same market issues are likely to be present? If there are likely to be repercussions for other jobs, it may be advisable for the market analysis to cover the job levels that fall above and below the job in question, or, if necessary, to cover the whole job family.

FIGURE 6.3 Benchmark job selection criteria

Selection criteria for benchmark jobs:

- Multiple incumbent jobs that cover a large proportion of the organization's employees (particularly useful when modelling pay structures);
- Ideally include jobs that are unlikely to change, so that repeat analyses can be conducted in future years;
- The selection should cover jobs where there is a realistic chance that comparable roles will be found externally;
- Ideally include a range of jobs that take into account the gender balance of the organization, so that potential bias in relation to predominantly male- or female-dominated jobs can be tested;
- If a new grade structure is being developed based on job evaluation, it helps if the choice of jobs for market analysis is similar to or the same as the selection of job evaluation benchmarks, as the combination of benchmark salary data and job evaluation scores for these jobs will inform grade structure development.

Alternatively if pay assessments need to be conducted for a range of jobs, for example to confirm the competitiveness of an existing pay structure or to create a new pay structure, it is necessary to get external benchmark data for a broad range of jobs spanning all levels and disciplines. Suggested selection criteria for benchmark jobs are listed in Figure 6.3.

Step 3: Defining data collection criteria

There are three main aspects to consider in defining what data to collect and where the data should be sourced from:

- Deciding who to compare against – what external market comparisons are appropriate?
- Deciding what data sources to use.
- Deciding which statistical reference points are appropriate, based on the market stance of the organization.

Defining the external comparison points

In discussing possible points of comparison with line managers or other stakeholders, there is often a wish to be very specific about comparator organizations. Where this is the case it may be necessary to persuade them that a small number of comparators does not typically represent the market for a job, and that a broader basis of comparison may give a more accurate representation of the market. The most appropriate external comparators are organizations that the organization loses people to and recruits from. This is likely to include organizations that are in the same sector for technical

FIGURE 6.4   Checklist: Choosing external comparators

Question	Response
Is there a reward policy that states the competitive stance of the organization?	
Is the external market for jobs sector specific? If so, are there likely to be enough external comparison points to enable comparisons to be made, or does it need to be broadened out to get a reasonable spread of data?	
Should the same external market reference points apply to all jobs across the organization? If not, have potential issues about internal consistency and equity been considered?	

or specialist jobs. However, it may be broader than this for roles that are transferable across organizations, such as finance, human resources, maintenance. Even where an organization's roles are transferable across organizations it is necessary to decide whether it is appropriate to compare across a broad range of sectors. For example, it is unlikely to be unrealistic for an organization providing social care services to compare its salaries against financial sector or blue-chip companies. In making this decision it is also necessary to consider whether the same points of external reference should apply across the whole organization, or whether there are distinct market pressures that need to be looked at separately. If different reference points are used in different parts of the organization, the organization will need to accept that if these data are used to determine pay, the organization will be putting more emphasis on external market than on internal equity. Figure 6.4 is a checklist for choosing external comparators.

Data sources

Having chosen the external market reference points, the next step is to consider data sources. There are many potential sources of market data and each can help to build a picture – but some are more helpful than others. Unfortunately there is no single source of market data that is complete and fully objective. However, an understanding of the sources will enable judgements to be made about the validity of the data. Potential data sources are listed in Figure 6.5, together with the issues that need to be taken into account in using them.

A salary survey conducted by a pay consultancy or research organization is likely to provide the most robust data for market analysis purposes. It is important to check the quality of the survey source before putting too much reliance on it. A checklist of what to look out for in a survey provider is provided in Figure 6.6.

FIGURE 6.5   Choosing data sources

Data source	Benefits	Data interpretation issues
UK government: Office for National Statistics (ONS)	Annual Survey of Hours and Earnings (ASHE) provides earnings statistics across the economy and based on broad occupational categories. The ONS also provides a national index of earnings increases. Both of these are valuable for tracking overall earnings trends.	The data are good for obtaining a high-level understanding of employment trends but are not specific enough to accurately benchmark individual jobs.
Reward research organizations such as IDS and XpertHR	The regular analyses provided by these organizations cover pay settlements for individual organizations as well as base pay settlement trends by sector. This can be valuable information for determining base pay budgets.	Information on pay structures and pay settlement rates may not be indicative of actual rates of pay received by individuals, depending on whether organizations' pay structures are fully reflective of how staff are paid in practice. The data tend to focus on overall rates of increase and pay for grade rather than specific jobs.
Network of local or sector contacts	Can be invaluable for informal checks or local benchmarking – particularly for lower-paid jobs, where pay levels may be strongly influenced by the local market.	Unless a local survey is conducted, the data may not be representative for the location as a whole and are unlikely to be representative of the sector.
The trade press	Can be a useful source and it may be helpful to keep a folder of relevant job adverts, but only for those adverts that quote specific salary or grade data (common in not-for-profit/public sector advertisements, but not for other sectors).	One or two job adverts are not likely to be representative of the market for a particular kind of job. Many adverts provide an indication of expected salary and what the organization may end up paying may or may not be close to the advertised salary.
Professional bodies	Some surveys are conducted with the support of professional survey bodies. May have strong credibility with line management.	There is a need to understand how the data have been collected. Some surveys are based on self-completed questionnaires received from a small sample of members, who change from year to year, so may not be representative of the profession.

FIGURE 6.5 *Continued*

Data source	Benefits	Data interpretation issues
Recruitment agencies	Can provide a good indication of the recruitment 'going rate' for the job rather than pay levels for those that are currently in job. Some agencies provide regular summary information on the state of the market or surveys.	Agency salary surveys reflect information supplied by job applicants and by information on applicants placed by the agency. The accuracy of these data is sometimes questionable. There may be a discrepancy between salaries of those in job and the recruitment market, due to recruitment premiums required to extract people from their current roles.
Annual reports	Useful for top-level positions in UK plcs, where the regulatory reporting framework requires top pay to be reported. These data are summarized in a number of commercially available surveys.	Some public sector bodies and not-for-profit sector organizations group pay data into bands and do not state which individuals the salaries apply to.
Salary surveys	A robustly conducted pay survey is likely to be the most valuable source of information.	Surveys can differ widely in the quality of information provided.

It may be the case that one survey provides sufficient data for analysing a job. However, in many cases it is helpful to have more than one data source to corroborate the data. In using different surveys any participant bias is likely to be discovered with use. For example, one survey might represent larger organizations; another might be stronger in one group of jobs or sector than others. Ideally, if regular use is made of market data, the organization should buy or participate in the same set of surveys over a number of years so that analyses can be replicated over time on a consistent basis. This is a more robust approach to market data analysis than 'cherry-picking' the source that has the most convenient answer at the time.

Defining the market stance

The other piece of information that is helpful in deciding what data to collect and who to collect them from is what market stance the organization applies. For example, does the organization aim to pay mid market against a chosen sector or group of companies? Or is there a need to have a more aggressive market stance? This may have been determined as part of the guiding reward principles or strategy.

FIGURE 6.6 Survey sources

Question	Response
Is the survey tailored to the relevant sector(s)?	
Does the survey include jobs/job levels that are representative of the job levels/types in your organization?	
Is the timing of the survey timely in relation to your own pay review? (As a rule of thumb, do not use surveys where the data are more than two years old.)	
Is the survey provider specific about the data input expected and the data standards that are applied in analysing the data?	
Are there good descriptions of the jobs and job levels? Is there a clear process for matching jobs into the survey?	
Does the survey provider clearly describe the standards applied in collecting and reporting data, including how base pay is defined (eg does it include regional allowances?), and how total cash is defined (eg does it include actual bonuses paid out in the last year, or target or maximum bonuses?)?	
Does the survey have a large enough sample to be representative?	
Does the survey provider quality-review the incoming data, to ensure accurate job matching?	
Does the survey have a consistent group of participants so that trends can be monitored from year to year?	
Does the survey provide information on how many participants have reported data for each job?	
Are different cuts of data provided according to scope factors that are relevant to the survey group (eg company turnover, location)?	
Does the survey provider provide, or enable participants to conduct, special analyses, eg through online data-interrogation capability?	

The rationale for positioning pay above mid-market levels may include:

- the need to accommodate a buoyant recruitment market;
- moving into new markets, so pay levels have to be pitched at a level that is attractive to people that already have the relevant skills;
- the need to recruit and retain in a rapidly growing organization.

In describing market positioning it is important to be explicit about what this means. For example, if it is said 'We pay *in* the upper quartile,' this has a different meaning to declaring that 'We pay *at* the upper quartile.' The former implies that the pay posture is between the 75 per cent level and the top of the market. The latter states a specific data reference point.

If the organization's market stance has been determined as part of an HR or reward strategy. this should help in determining what needs to be collected for different elements of the reward package, with respect to any or all of the following:

- base pay;
- total cash (base pay plus bonuses and allowances);
- total remuneration (as above plus benefits);
- total reward (as for total remuneration plus intangible aspects of reward such as learning and development opportunities and the work environment).

Where there is no clear stance on pay competitiveness, it will be necessary to decide which statistical points to collect data on. Where this is the case, the collection of median and upper quartile data will usually provide a reasonable spread for decision-making purposes.

A common question relating to survey data is whether the mean or median is a better reflection of mid-market data. Generally, the median is preferred because it represents the absolute middle of the data spread. Where a survey provides both mean and median, the difference between the two will indicate skews in the data. If there is a significant difference between the two it may mean that the data have not been validated effectively, that there is a small sample or that there are significantly higher or lower payers in the marketplace.

Step 4: Matching jobs to the external market

Most surveys use similar criteria for matching jobs. This includes a combination of some or all of the headings listed in Figure 6.7.

Due to the limitations on what data can be realistically collected, expectations need to be set with line managers to make them aware that differences in the way that a job is done, or nuances in the tasks and responsibilities from one organization to the next are unlikely to show up in market data. On the other hand, more specific comparison between jobs may be possible if the organization conducts its own survey, or if it participates in a tailored sector or job specific survey.

FIGURE 6.7 Job matching criteria

Data required	Comments
Function or job family (eg finance)	
Job title (eg head of)	
Summary job or level profile	
Organization or reporting level (a description of the level that the job operates at, eg mid manager or experienced specialist typically reporting to function head, requiring experience in...)	
Organization scope factors such as revenue, total number of employees or sector-specific scope factors	
Location	
Job evaluation scores – where surveys are related to specific job evaluation schemes	

Step 5: Analysing and interpreting data

This section addresses some of the most common issues that come up in data analysis.

Number of data sources

A guiding rule is that more sources does not necessarily mean better. However, it is important to be clear about what sources have been used when discussing findings with colleagues internally.

In analysing data there are two types of market assessment. The first is a straightforward cut or 'drawdown' of data from a single source. This may include single or multiple regression analyses, which indicate the line of best fit between scope parameters for the jobs (such as company turnover) and pay levels.

A drawdown from a single source may be sufficient where there is one reliable source of data, for example where the data are drawn from a sector-specific survey or tailored to the organization. Where this is the case the statistics can be quoted directly.

However, in many cases a single data source will not be sufficient. Where this is so, it is necessary to gather and interpret data from a range of sources to formulate an assessment.

Where a range of sources is used it is important to collect and record data systematically. An example format for a data record sheet is provided in Figure 6.8. This includes:

FIGURE 6.8 Example data analysis record

Survey and date of survey	Survey job title	Sample size	Scope data (eg company revenue)	Statistics	Base £	Total cash (if different)	% update factor	Updated base
XYZ survey: data as at 1/4/10	Finance manager level 13 (ie head of function reporting to director)	36	National (exc London) £20–£50m turnover services sector	Median 75th %	63,000 69,000	64,500 72,000	N/A	N/A
ABC survey: data as at 1/9/09	Head of finance; not director level: ref Survey job match description 34	61	All (can't separate out London): £20–£50m turnover 500–1,000 staff	Median 75th % Median 75th %	60,000 74,000 59,500 63,000	65,000 79,000 61,700 73,000	3% 3%	61,800 76,220 61,285 64,890
etc				Median 75th %				

- The survey source and the effective date of the survey data (not the publication date of the survey, which may be several months later).
- The job title and any other data that help to fix the quality of the survey match; in recording data, over-reliance on matching jobs against job titles is risky. Any reputable survey will have a defined job matching process, eg to definitions of organizational level, summary job or job-family-level profiles or to a job evaluation profile.
- The relevant survey statistics split into base pay and total cash.
- Columns to record and incorporate data adjustments to bring them up to date if needed.

This format can be refined to include additional information, such as benefits, as needed.

This data analysis record should be filed, whether electronically or manually, so that the market evidence can be retrieved and questions addressed. Ready access to previous assessments means that a record of the data sources used is available for reference from one year to the next, making it straightforward to replicate the analysis in future years.

Understanding regional and local pay differences

One of the most difficult issues to deal with in interpreting survey data is how to treat perceived regional differentials. Surveys consistently show clear pay differentials between London, the South East and elsewhere. However, the pattern is far less clear for other locations. Even where surveys suggest regional pay differences, the pattern of such differences within the same survey may not always be consistent from one year to the next and may be due to sample size and profile differences rather than genuine regional differentials. It is therefore important to look at the regional sample size, as differences in data may be more reflective of this and who the regional employers are. It is therefore advisable to base any regional analysis on both historical and current survey data to check whether regional differences are consistent over time. If not, it is advisable to rely on national data.

Regional surveys will be relevant for organizations based in London or the South East, as both regions have a distinctive pay profile. In other regions the regional surveys are likely to be more relevant for lower-level jobs, where the markets are more localized. However, it is important to note that many large employers operate a national pay structure (outside London and the South East), so it may still be appropriate to use national data. On the other hand, some employers allow flexibility to adapt to local market rates, which do not necessarily reflect a regional pay differential but specific local demands. This is unlikely to show up in a regional survey.

The total reward package

Base pay may not be whole picture – even for junior-level jobs. Base pay may be supplemented by profit sharing and/or performance-related bonuses/commission, based on any combination of individual, team and company performance. If a true comparison of actual earnings is needed it is therefore appropriate to compare total cash levels.

Most surveys include base pay and total cash, but few provide a comprehensive overview of benefits, and only a handful of surveys attempt to generate a total remuneration comparison including pay and the value/cost of all benefits. However, it is these items that might make the difference in overall competitiveness. For example, differences in holiday entitlement or pension provision may have a significant impact on overall competitiveness. Even though few surveys provide a total remuneration value, they will often provide summary information about pay practices and policies. Where this is the case it is important to review this and to make notes about any differences between the typical total remuneration package for the survey sample compared with your organization.

Incumbent- vs. organization-weighted data

One of the less obvious features of survey reports is whether data are being reported on an individual incumbent basis (incumbent weighted) or whether the data from each participating organization are counted as a single piece of data (company weighted). Incumbent-weighted data show the true marketplace with respect to the total pool of job holders among the survey participants. Company-weighted data indicate organizational competitiveness. Some surveys have a hybrid approach, that allows organizations to report all incumbents up to a certain number and then to provide representative actual incumbent data within that limit.

Some surveys base their analysis on grade ranges and mid-points. Although this can provide useful information about pay structures, it does not reflect what people actually earn. This may be useful information in designing a salary structure, but it should be treated with caution if the aim is to compare actual pay levels.

Deciding on the 'going rate' for the job

The purpose of analysing the external market is usually to come up with a market range or figure that is representative of the chosen market stance.

In making this decision it is important not to simply average together every piece of data that has been recorded. Increasing familiarity with the survey sources will inform a view about which sources are better than others. Ideally there should be one or two main sources, with any additional data being used to confirm and validate these primary sources. This may mean narrowing down the range of existing data sources to a small number of reliable surveys.

If the sample is small, the reliability of the data is more questionable than for a large sample, except if the data relate to a very specific field of work. Reputable survey providers will provide information on the sample size for each job and will apply standards relating to the minimum sample allowed for each job reported (typically a minimum sample of at least five for reporting mean and median, and nine for quartiles). Information about the sample size helps when forming a view about what weight to place on each piece of data.

Another consideration is whether data need to be aged to reflect current salary levels. This may be necessary where the survey was conducted some time ago, or if the analysis will only be used at a future date. To assess whether data should be aged it is necessary to know the effective date of data submission (survey providers usually require data to be submitted in respect of a specific date), and when most survey participants have their pay reviews. In some sectors organizations tend to have a similar review date, eg between January and April in the voluntary sector. For all analyses conducted in the following spring the survey results based on data collated in the previous summer will therefore need to be aged forward by a year to reflect the new pay cycle, even though a full year has not yet passed. However, where pay reviews are evenly spread over the year, it may be appropriate to age the data on a monthly basis from the effective date of the survey.

The amount to age data by can usually be derived from data on current and projected pay settlements. Alternatively the survey provider may provide an estimated uplift. Pay research firms such as IDS and XpertHR are helpful providers of pay settlement trends and projections across all industry sectors.

What to do when there are weak external data

There will always be jobs where good survey data are not available. Where this is the case there are three choices:

- Get as close a match as possible, based on the elements of the job that can be compared externally, such as skills or experience, reporting level or function.
- Rely instead on internal pay relationships. For example, project management roles could be compared against jobs that incumbents have moved from or are likely to move back into; or compare against jobs with comparable job evaluation scores, where applicable.
- Conduct a tailored pay survey.

The choice depends on how critical the job is and the expected return from the effort needed to seek out more data.

Validating an assessment

A quality check should be conducted on the findings that are emerging. It can be helpful to check the data for one job against similar jobs, for example those above and below it in the same career pathway. If the outcome is not what is expected, consider why. For example, was the survey match against the right level of job? Are the survey data sufficiently robust? Can the assessment be corroborated with other sources?

Step 6: Presenting results

Whether or not there is a need to report formally on the market assessments will depend on what the data will be used for. For example, if the analysis is being used to create a grade structure it is likely that the findings will be plugged directly into the grade modelling exercise. However, where findings need to be reported back to line management, it is necessary to think about how to present the data.

Where data are drawn from a range of surveys, care must be taken in describing what the analysis represents. For example, the analysis can refer to a 'mid-market' assessment – but not the median or mean, as the figures reported will not be true statistics, except where they are aggregated into a single database.

The format will depend on the reason for conducting the analysis in the first place. Examples of simple tables for presenting findings are given in Figures 6.9 to 6.11.

FIGURE 6.9   Market assessment report: example 1

Job	1 Current salary £	2 Public sector mid-market basic salary £	1 as % of 2	3 Commercial sector mid-market basic salary £	1 as % of 3	Notes on job match
Head of publications	58,000	44,000	123	46,000	117	Head of publications working at senior function head level, equivalent to director
Deputy editor	29,800	31,000	96	32,000	93	Senior/deputy editor with direct editorial responsibility for one or more publications
Editorial assistant	27,000	25,500	106	26,000	103	Assistant editor with at least two–three years' editorial and production experience

FIGURE 6.10   Market assessment report: example 2

Role	Costco actual base pay (A) £	Competitive assessment (B) £	Costco as % of assessment (A as % of B mid point) %
Operations manager	70,300	68,000–72,000	100
Personnel manager	46,700	48,000–52,000	93
Area manager	42,000	35,500–39,500	112

FIGURE 6.11   Market assessment report: example 3

Job	Current band	Current band range (inc London allowance) £	Mid-market base pay commercial sector £	Bonus target commercial sector	Mid-market base pay public/not-for-profit sector £	Notes on job match
Manager, central services	N/A new job	N/A	50,000	10–20%	45,000	1
Media relations manager	1	31,800–48,900	52,000	10–20%	51,500	2
Facilities team leader	2	23,800–37,500	31,000	0–10%	31,000	3

Using market analysis internally requires careful communication to put it into context. It is a means to an end and is unlikely to be the final answer. The purpose of market data is to support the decision-making process, not to replace the need for it. The checklist in Figure 6.12 is an example of a full description of the factors taken into account in conducting and interpreting the assessment.

FIGURE 6.12   Checklist: factors taken into account in conducting and interpreting a market rate assessment

---

Checklist: example market analysis explanation

A full explanation will include:
- How the primary factors influencing pay levels have been taken into account, ie:
  - industry sector
  - the annual income/revenue of the organization, or other relevant scope data.
- The level, function and content of the job; it is also helpful to provide notes on job match with the assessments, so that the line manager can form their own view about the quality of job match, particularly if there is no direct match with the external market.
- The extent to which location has been taken into account in the assessments.
- A reminder of the organization's stated market pay posture.
- A statement that the analysis of pay data is not an exact science and that the analysis includes a degree of judgment about the market data. Pay assessments provide benchmark information to support judgments, not a set of recommendations in respect of what the organization should pay.
- Whether the data have been aged forward to reflect current pay levels.
- A comment to the effect that it will be possible to find organizations that pay more than the figures indicated in the assessment; in particular, a market premium may apply for new appointments. However, individual examples of high recruitment salaries are not a sound foundation on which to judge the overall competitiveness of the organization's pay posture.
- Depending on the purpose of the assessment, it may be helpful to describe what margin of tolerance there is in interpreting a pay assessment, for example a job may be regarded as being competitively paid against the market assessment if the incumbent's actual pay falls within a 10% range either side of the assessment. This recognizes that a number of factors influence actual pay levels, including time in job, performance and experience, and that judgment has to be applied in interpreting the pay data.
- Whether the rest of the organization's benefits and terms and conditions are broadly comparable with the external market; if not, the extent to which it may be appropriate to make some adjustment to reflect the difference.

References

e-reward market data tool: www.e-reward.co.uk
Incomes Data Services: www.incomesdata.co.uk
Office for Government Statistics: www.ons.gov.uk.
XpertHR: www.xperthr.co.uk

Tool 07
Base pay management

Introduction

Base pay management is the process of deciding on pay levels, developing grade and pay structures and operating the financial reward system. It is concerned with the rate for the job as affected by its value to the organization and its market rate. However, rate for the person considerations are taken into account when provision is made in a pay structure for pay progression related to performance, contribution or service.

Base pay management is therefore at the core of reward management. It involves the use of job evaluation and market rate analysis techniques. It is concerned with methods of pay progression within pay structures and is therefore linked to the design and management of contingent pay schemes such as performance pay. It also deals with the operation of pay reviews.

Graded pay structures are a fundamental aspect of base pay management. However, many organizations, especially smaller ones, do not have a formal structure and rely on 'spot rates' (rates for jobs that do not allow any scope for the progression of base pay). Spot rates are also frequently used for the base pay of top management posts where they tend to be rates for the person rather than rates for the job, although there is likely to be scope for the payment of additional cash bonuses.

Purpose of the tool

This tool focuses on the design of the most common form of grade and pay structures, namely: graded, broad-branded, career family and job family grade and pay structures. Other aspects of base pay management are covered in the tools dealing with job evaluation, market rate analysis, performance pay and pay reviews.

Contents of the tool

The tool contains the following sections:

- The grade and pay structure design sequence;
- Analysis of present arrangements;
- Choice of structure;
- Selection and development of job evaluation scheme;
- Definition of guiding principles;
- Design options;
- Graded pay structure design;
- Broad-banded structure design;
- Career family structure design;
- Job family structure design;
- Assimilation policy;
- Protection policy;
- Implementation.

The grade and pay structure design sequence

FIGURE 7.1   The grade and pay structure design sequence

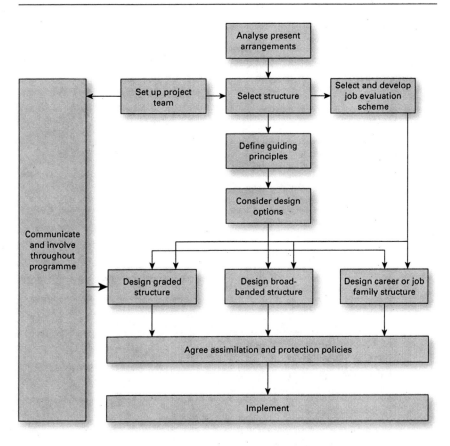

Analysis of present arrangements

Line managers, staff and staff representatives should be involved in an analysis of the present arrangement to indicate where changes may have to be made. The analysis could be based on the questionnaire set out in Figure 7.2. Use could be made of surveys, special workshops or focus groups, or it could be discussed in a consultative committee.

FIGURE 7.2   Analysis of present grade and pay structure arrangements

	Statement	Fully agree	Partly agree	Partly disagree	Fully disagree
1	The present grade and pay structure is quite satisfactory.				
2	We have no problems in grading jobs within the structure.				
3	There are too many anomalies (under or over-graded jobs).				
4	The structure no longer fits the way work is organized.				
5	Pay levels are competitive.				
6	The structure is easy to manage and control.				
7	The structure provides adequate scope for pay progression.				
8	The structure does not contribute to the creation of a gender gap.				
9	The structure is inflexible.				
10	People generally understand and accept how their jobs are graded.				

Choice of structure

Assuming that the analysis indicates that radical action is required, a choice needs to be made of which type of structure is appropriate. The choice can be based on an analysis of the features and advantages and disadvantages of different structures as summarized in Figure 7.3 and an assessment of the criteria for when they are appropriate (Figure 7.4).

FIGURE 7.3　Summary description of different grade and pay structures

Type of structure	Features	Advantages	Disadvantages
Narrow-graded	A sequence of job grades: 10 or more Narrow pay ranges, eg 20%–40% Progression usually linked to performance	Clearly indicate pay relativities Facilitate control Easy to understand	Create hierarchical rigidity Prone to grade drift Inappropriate in a delayered organization
Broad-graded	A sequence of between six and nine grades Fairly broad pay ranges, eg 40%–50% Progression linked to contribution and may be controlled by thresholds or zones	As for narrow-graded structures but in addition: The broader grades can be defined more clearly Better control can be exercised over grade drift	Too much scope for pay progression Control mechanisms can be provided but they can be difficult to manage May be costly
Broad-banded	A series of, often, five or six 'broad' bands Wide pay bands – typically between 50% and 80% Progression linked to contribution and competence and may be controlled by thresholds or zones	More flexible Reward lateral development and growth in competence Fit non-hierarchical organizations	Create unrealistic expectations of scope for pay rises Seem to restrict scope for promotion Difficult to understand Equal pay problems
Career family	Career families identified and defined Career paths defined for each family in terms of key activities and competence requirements Same grade and pay structure for each family	Clarify career paths within and between families Facilitate the achievement of equity between families and therefore equal pay Facilitate level definitions	Could be difficult to manage May *appear* to be divisive if 'silos' emerge
Job family	Separate grade and pay structures for job families containing similar jobs Progression linked to competence and/or contribution	May inhibit lateral career development May be difficult to maintain internal equity between job families unless underpinned by job evaluation	Facilitate pay differentiation between market groups Define career paths against clear criteria Can appear to be divisive
Pay spine	A series of incremental pay points covering all jobs Grades may be superimposed Progression linked to service	Easy to manage Pay progression not based on managerial judgment	No scope for differentiating rewards according to performance May be costly as staff drift up the spine Length of service related increases may not be justifiable

FIGURE 7.4   Criteria for assessing the extent to which a structure is appropriate

Type of structure	The structure is more likely to be appropriate when:
Narrow-graded	The organization is large and bureaucratic, with well defined and extended hierarchies.
	Pay progression is expected to occur in small but relatively frequent steps.
	The culture is one in which much significance is attached to status as indicated by gradings.
	When some but not too much scope for pay progression is wanted.
Broad-graded	It is believed that if there is a relatively limited number of grades it will be possible to define and therefore differentiate them more accurately as an aid to better precision when grading jobs.
	An existing narrow-graded structure is the main cause of grade drift because the structure cannot accommodate market factors.
	A broad-banded structure has led to pay drift due to lack of management control.
	It is considered that pay progression through grades can be related to contribution and that it is possible to introduce effective control mechanisms.
Broad-banded	Greater flexibility in pay determination and management is required.
	It is believed that job evaluation should no longer drive grading decisions, greater attention being paid to market value.
	The bands are used purely to define career levels rather than pay opportunity.
	The focus is on rewarding people for lateral development.
	The organization has been delayered.
Career family	There are distinct families and different career paths within and between families can be identified and defined.
	There is a strong emphasis on career development in the organization.
	Robust methods of defining professional, specialist and technical competencies exist.
	It is believed to be inappropriate to vary pay structures between families.
Job family	As for career families plus:
	There are distinct market groups that need to be rewarded differently.
	The range of responsibility and the basis upon which levels exist vary between families.
Pay spine	This is the traditional approach in a public or voluntary sector organization and it fits the culture.
	It is believed to be impossible to measure different levels of contribution fairly and consistently and length of service is therefore the best criterion.
	Ease of administration is an important consideration.

Selection and development of job evaluation scheme

A point-factor analytical job evaluation scheme is often applied when designing a graded structure, although it may be limited to the initial design of the structure with analytical job matching being used to grade jobs. This approach is used less often in the design of broad-banded or career/job family structures, where the most common method is to make a provisional advance decision on the number of bands or career/job family levels, and then position roles in bands (often by reference to market rates) or allocate roles into defined levels by analytical matching. Job evaluation may only be deployed at a later stage to validate the positioning of roles in bands or the allocation of jobs to family levels, to check on relativities and, sometimes, to define the bands or levels in job evaluation score terms.

A non-analytical job classification scheme is sometimes used to define grades or bands and provide the basis for non-analytical matching, ie slotting jobs into a grade or band using job descriptions and grade definitions that have not been specifically analysed into factors, although reference may be made in broad terms to such job characteristics as level of responsibility.

Definition of guiding principles

Guiding principles for the design of the grade and pay structure need to be defined at this stage. An example of a set of guiding principles is given in Figure 7.5.

FIGURE 7.5 Example: grade and pay structure guiding principles

---

Grade and pay structures should:
- be appropriate to the culture, characteristics and needs of the organization and its employees;
- facilitate the management of relativities and the achievement of equity, fairness, consistency and transparency in managing gradings and pay;
- be capable of adapting to pressures arising from market rate changes and skill shortages;
- facilitate operational flexibility and continuous development;
- provide scope as required for rewarding performance, contribution and increases in skill and competence;
- clarify reward, lateral development and career opportunities;
- be constructed logically and clearly so that the basis upon which they operate can readily be communicated to employees;
- enable the organization to exercise control over the implementation of pay policies and budgets.

It is also necessary to ensure that the pay structure is non-discriminatory by following the principles set out in Figure 7.6.

FIGURE 7.6   Avoiding discrimination in grade and pay structures

- Take great care over grade boundary decisions – the aim should be to avoid placing them between jobs that have been evaluated as virtually indistinguishable, bearing in mind that the problem will be most acute if grade boundaries are placed between traditionally male and female jobs (in any situation where such boundary problems exist it is good practice to re-evaluate the jobs, possibly using a direct 'comparable worth' or equal-value approach, which concentrates on the particular jobs).
- Ensure that 'read-across' mechanisms exist between different job families and occupational groups if they are not all covered by the same plan.
- Treat market rate comparisons with caution to ensure that differentials arising from market forces can be objectively justified.
- Take care over the implementation of the pay structure to ensure that female employees (indeed, any employees) are not disadvantaged by the methods used to adjust their pay following regrading.
- Use a non-discriminatory analytical job evaluation system to define grade boundaries and grade jobs.
- Do not use discriminatory job descriptions as a basis for designing and managing the structure.
- Ensure that men's or women's jobs do not cluster respectively at the higher and lower levels in the grade of the hierarchy.
- Ensure that any variation between pay levels for men and women in similarly evaluated jobs (for example for market rate reasons) can be objectively justified.
- Ensure that red-circling is free of gender bias.
- Ensure that there are objectively justifiable reasons for any inconsistency in the relation of the grading of jobs in the structure to job evaluation results.

Design options

Whichever structure is selected, there will be a number of design options. These comprise the number of grades, bands or levels, the width of the grades (the span of pay ranges), the differentials between grades, the degree to which there should be overlap between grades, if any, and the method of pay progression within grades. In broad-banded and some broad-graded structures there is also choice on the infrastructure (the use of reference points or zones). In career or job family structures there are options concerning the number of families, the composition of families and the basis upon which levels should be defined. The options are summarized in Figure 7.7.

FIGURE 7.7   Grade and pay structure design options

Design feature	Design considerations
Number of grades, levels or bands	The range and types of roles to be covered by the structure. The range of pay and job evaluation points scores to be accommodated. The number of levels in the organizational hierarchy (this will be an important factor in a broad-banded structure). Decisions on where grade boundaries should be placed following a job evaluation exercise that has produced a ranked order of jobs – this might identify the existence of clearly defined clusters of jobs at the various levels in the hierarchy between which there are significant differences in job size. The potential for 'grade drift' (unjustified upgradings in response to pressure, lack of promotion opportunities or because job evaluation has been applied laxly), which can be increased if there are too many narrow grades.
Pay range spans	Views on the scope that should be allowed for performance, contribution or career progression within grade. Equal pay considerations – wide spans, especially extended incremental scales, are a major cause of pay gaps between men and women because women, who are more likely to have career breaks than men, may not have the same opportunity as men to progress to the upper regions of the range. In a broad-banded structure, the range of market rates and job evaluation scores covering the jobs allocated to the band.
Differentials between pay ranges	Differentials between pay ranges should provide scope to recognize increases in job size between successive grades. If differentials are too close – less than 10% – many jobs become borderline cases, which can result in a proliferation of appeals and arguments about grading. Large differentials below senior management level of more than 25 per cent can create problems for marginal or borderline cases because of the amount at stake. In most organizations with conventional grade structures a differential of between 15% and 20% is appropriate except, perhaps, at the highest levels.
Pay range overlap	There is a choice on whether or not pay ranges should overlap and if so, by how much. Large overlaps can create equal pay problems if men are clustered at the top of their grades and women are at the lower end.
Pay progression	There is a choice of methods of pay progression between the various forms of contingent pay, namely performance, competence or contribution-related as described in Tool 8 and the fixed service-related increments common in the public sector.

Graded pay structure design

A graded pay structure involves first designing the grade structure and then deciding on the pay ranges that should be attached to it.

The two approaches to design the grade structure are:

- the derived method in which decisions on the grade structure are led by point-factor job evaluation;
- the pre-emptive method, in which the number of grades is determined first and each grade is then defined as a basis for analytical matching or market pricing.

The derived method (use of point-factor job evaluation)

The derived method consists of the following steps:

1 Use point-factor job evaluation to produce a rank order of jobs according to their job evaluation scores.

2 Either take a preliminary view on the preferred number of grades or analyse the rank order to establish by inspection where jobs might be grouped into grades and how many grades emerge from this procedure.

3 Decide where the boundaries that will define grades should be placed in the rank order (guidelines on defining boundaries are given in Figure 7.8).

4 Remember that, as far as possible, the grade boundaries in the rank order should divide groups or clusters of jobs that are significantly different in size so that all the jobs placed in a grade are clearly smaller than the jobs in the next higher grade and larger than the jobs placed in the next lower grade.

The grades in a structure established in this manner can be defined in the form of grade profiles using the job evaluation factors as the headings for each profile. These can form the basis for analytical matching.

The pre-emptive method

The pre-emptive method takes place in the following steps:

1 Assume number of grades. The assumption on how many grades are required is based on an analysis of the existing hierarchy of roles and a judgement on how many levels are needed to produce a logical grouping of those roles, level by level. A logical grouping is one in which each grade contains roles whose levels are broadly comparable in terms of responsibility and decision making and there is a step difference in the degree of responsibility between each level.

FIGURE 7.8 Method of deciding on grade boundaries

Analyse the rank order to identify any significant gaps in the points scores between adjacent jobs. These natural breaks in points scores will then constitute the boundaries between clusters of jobs that can be allocated to adjacent grades. This is the preferred approach but in many cases there will be no significant gaps. If so, the following method can be used:

- Jobs with common features as indicated by the job evaluation factors are grouped together so that a distinction can be made between the characteristics of the jobs in different grades – it should be possible to demonstrate that the jobs grouped into one grade resemble each other more than they resemble jobs placed in adjacent grades.
- The grade hierarchy should take account of the organizational hierarchy, ie jobs in which the job holder reports to a higher-level job holder should be placed in a lower grade, although this principle should not be followed slavishly when an organization is over-hierarchical with, perhaps, a series of one-over-one reporting relationships.
- There would need to be good justification for placing any boundaries between jobs mainly carried out by men and jobs mainly carried out by women.
- Caution should be exercised in placing any boundaries immediately above jobs in which large numbers of people are employed, because this may result in a large number of appeals against the grading.
- The grade width in terms of job evaluation points should represent a significant step in demands on job holders as indicated by the job evaluation scheme.

2 Define grades. There is choice between a simple non-analytical or semi-analytical job classification approach and a full analytical approach. A non-analytical job classification approach involves preparing an overall definition of the grade to enable 'job slotting' to take place. This means slotting 'whole jobs', ie ones that have not been analysed under job evaluation factor headings, into grades by comparing the whole job description with grade. A full analytical approach involves the preparation of grade profiles. These use job evaluation factors as the headings for the profile of each grade, which can be compared with role profiles set out under the same headings so that analytical matching can take place.

3 Revise initial assumption as necessary. The process of definition may reveal that the number of grades assumed to be required initially was either too many (the distinctions between them could not be made with sufficient clarity) or too few (it becomes apparent that the range of roles to be fitted into the structure was too great to be accommodated into the number of grades available). If this is the case, the number of grades would have to be adjusted iteratively until a satisfactory result is obtained.

4 Match benchmark roles. The benchmark roles are matched to grades in accordance with a predetermined analytical matching protocol as described in the job evaluation tool. When matched, the information on the benchmark roles may suggest changes to the grade profiles.

5 Match remaining roles. The remaining roles can be matched to the grade profiles, using the protocol. A confirmation of the match can be obtained by comparing them with the graded benchmark roles.

Pay range design

The steps required to determine pay ranges are:

1 Obtain information on the market rates for benchmark jobs where available. If possible, this should indicate the median rate and the upper and lower quartiles. Remember that there may be some key jobs for which market rate data are not available.

2 List the jobs placed within each grade on the basis of job evaluation (these might be limited to benchmark jobs that have been evaluated, but there must be an adequate number of them if a proper basis for the design is to be provided).

3 Establish the actual rates of pay of the job holders.

4 For each grade set out the range of pay for job holders and calculate their average or median rate of pay (the pay practice point). It is helpful to plot this pay practice data as illustrated in Figure 7.9, which shows pay in each grade against job evaluation scores and includes a pay practice trend line.

5 Agree policy on how the organization's pay levels should relate to market rates – its 'market stance'. This could be at the median, or above the median if it is believed that pay levels should be more competitive.

6 Calculate the average market rates for the benchmark jobs in each grade according to pay stance policy, eg the median rates. This produces the range market reference point.

7 Compare the practice and market reference points in each range and decide on the range reference point. This usually becomes the mid point of the pay range for the grade and is regarded as the competitive rate for a fully competent job holder in that grade. This is a judgemental process that takes into account the difference between the practice and policy points, the perceived need to be more competitive if policy rates are higher, and the likely costs of increasing rates.

8 Examine the pay differentials between reference points in adjacent grades. These should provide scope to recognize increases in job size, and, so far as possible, variations between differentials should be kept to a minimum. If differentials are too close – less than 10 per cent – many jobs become borderline cases, which can result in a proliferation of appeals and arguments about grading. Large differentials below senior management level of more than

FIGURE 7.9 Scattergram of evaluations and pay

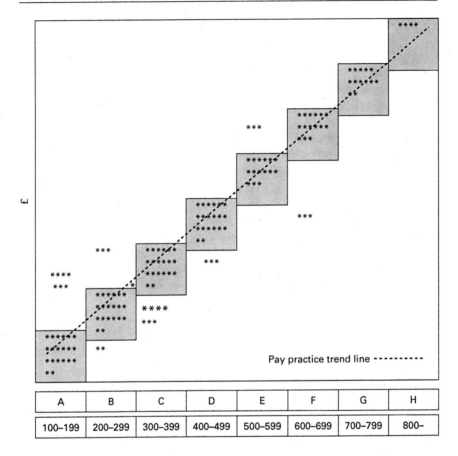

A	B	C	D	E	F	G	H
100–199	200–299	300–399	400–499	500–599	600–699	700–799	800–

25 per cent can create problems for marginal or borderline cases because of the amount at stake. Experience has shown that in most organizations with conventional grade structures a differential of between 15 and 20 per cent is appropriate except, perhaps, at the highest levels.

9 Decide on the range of pay around the reference point, eg 20 per cent on either side of the reference point. Thus if that point is 100 per cent, the range is from 80 per cent to 120 per cent. The range will, however, vary in accordance with policy on the scope for progression, and if a given range of pay has to be covered by the structure, the fewer the grades the wider the ranges.

10 Decide on the extent, if any, to which pay ranges should overlap. Overlap recognizes that an experienced job holder at the top of a range may be making a greater contribution than an inexperienced job holder at the lower end of the range above. Large overlaps can

create equity issues between jobs that have the same salary but are in different grades. This is particularly pronounced if it means that individuals with the same pay could fit within more than two grades.

11 Review the impact of the above pay range decisions on the pay of existing staff in order to calculate implementation costs. Establish the number of staff whose present rate of pay is above or below the pay range for the grade into which their jobs have been placed and the extent of the difference between the rate of pay of those below the minimum and the lowest point of that pay range. Calculate the costs of bringing them up to the minimum. Pay-modelling software or Excel spreadsheets can be used for this purpose.

12 When the above steps have been completed it may be necessary to review the decisions made on the grade structure and pay reference points and ranges, especially when the costs calculated in stage 11 are too high. Iteration is almost always necessary to obtain a satisfactory result that conforms to the criteria for grade and pay structures mentioned earlier and minimizes the cost of implementation. Alternatives can be modelled using the software mentioned above.

Broad-banded structure design

Broad-banded structures are easier to design than graded structures and they cost less to implement – fewer anomalies will be created because the existing rates of pay of a higher proportion of people will be within the wide spans of the limited number of bands. However, implementation may be more challenging because of the requirement for a high degree of management decision making in relation to the external market and performance or contribution.

The steps required to design a broad-banded structure are:

1 Decide on objectives. The objectives of the structure should be set out in terms of what it is expected to achieve; for example: increase flexibility in the provision of rewards, especially in responding to market rate pressures, reflect organization structure, provide a better base for rewarding lateral development and growth in competency, eliminate or at least reduce the need for job evaluation, replace an over-complex and inappropriate grade and pay structure.

2 Decide on number of bands. The decision on the number of bands will be based on an analysis of the existing organization structure and hierarchy of jobs. The aim is to identify the value-adding tiers that exist in the business. An initial assessment may be made, for example, that there are five tiers, comprising: senior managers;

middle managers; first-line managers and specialists; senior administrators and support staff; administrators and support staff. This structure should be regarded as provisional at this stage – it could be changed after the more detailed work in the next two stages.

3 Decide on band architecture. A decision has to be made at this stage on the use of anchor points and zones. If anchor points are to be used, which is most often the case, the method of determining where they should be placed in bands (by market pricing, job evaluation, or both) should be decided. If zones are to be used, decisions need to be made on the width of the zones and the basis upon which people should progress within and between zones.

4 Define the bands. Bands can be defined in one of the following ways:
   - descriptive labels: the generic roles that have been allocated to bands;
   - outline generic descriptions of jobs in the bands;
   - summary analytical description of bands;
   - extended analytical description of bands;
   - in terms of a range of job evaluation points.

5 Incorporate job families. It may be decided to divide each band into job families so that the relativities within the band and the relationship to external rates can be treated separately and the career path within a band can be identified for the separate families.

6 Prepare role profiles for benchmark jobs. Identify benchmark jobs that are representative of different functions at the levels covered by the structure and for which market price data can be obtained. They should include as many of the key generic roles as possible. Role profiles for each of them are then prepared. The profiles should provide sufficient information to enable them to be matched with the band definitions and for use in market comparisons.

7 Match the benchmark roles to the bands. The matching process should provisionally allocate each benchmark role to a band. It is best carried out by a team consisting of line managers and employee representatives, facilitated by HR or an outside consultant. This initial matching may indicate that the bands need to be redefined.

8 Obtain market prices. Conduct surveys and/or access pay information databases to establish the market rates of the benchmark roles.

9 Decide on reference points. Assuming a decision has been made to have reference points and zones, decide on the reference points for the benchmark roles. These may be based entirely on market rates, but internal relativities as determined by job evaluation may be taken into account.

10 Decide on zones. Assuming a decision has been made to use zones, these should now be attached to the reference points for the benchmark roles in accordance with the policy determined at stage 3.

11 Define pay ranges of bands. This is usually done empirically by reference to the earlier decisions on reference points and zones – the range of pay for a band will be the range of pay from the bottom of the lowest zone in the band to the top of the highest zone.

12 Define bands in terms of job evaluation scores. If the benchmark roles have been evaluated, this will indicate the bracket of job evaluation scores that can be used to define each band, which might provide a guide to allocating non-benchmark or new roles to bands.

13 Allocate non-benchmark roles to bands. The remaining non-benchmark jobs are allocated to bands by analytical matching or, less desirably, by whole-job slotting.

14 Communicate outcomes. Staff should have been involved and kept informed of the progress of the design process throughout the exercise but in this final stage the way in which broad-banding works and how it will affect them should be explained in detail.

Career family structure design

The steps required to design a career family structure are:

1 Select and define career families. Decide on what career families are required. Typically, not more than four or five families are identified. The choice of families is between functions (eg marketing, finance) or activities (eg administration, support staff), or a combination of functions and activities.

2 Decide on number of levels in the career family structure and define them with level profiles. Level profiles are required that apply to all the families in the structure, bearing in mind that the defining characteristic of a career family is that the levels and the pay ranges attached to them are common to all the families in the structure (as distinct from job family structures in which levels and ranges differ between some or all of the families).

3 Identify, define and match benchmark roles. A representative sample of benchmark roles is identified, defined as role profiles and matched with the level profiles as described above for a graded structure.

4 Conduct analytical matching. Analytical matching procedures are used to allocate the remaining roles to levels. It is advisable to test the process first in one family – this will not only test the procedure but will also enable model career family structures to be used when dealing with the other career families.

5 Attach pay ranges to levels. Pay ranges are established for each level as described above for graded structures.

6 Validate relativities between career families. The allocation of jobs to levels through matching across the career families is validated by reference to job evaluation scores to ensure that the relativities between them look reasonable. Some adjustment may need to be made as a result of this cross-check if it exposes inequities between families.

Job family structure design

The process of designing job family structures is essentially the same as that used for career family structures. The difference is that, because some individual families will have their own pay and level structure, the analysis of market rates and the organization of work in families will have a stronger influence on the design.

Assimilation policy

It is necessary to have a policy on where staff will be assimilated to the new structure. This is usually at their existing salary or, in the case of a revised pay spine, on the nearest point in a new incremental scale above their existing salary. The following categories of staff will need to be covered by the policy:

- Employees with current pay and pay potential both within the new pay range. This group is the easiest to deal with and the majority of staff will normally be included in it.

- Employees whose current pay is within the new pay range but their pay potential is higher than new maximum. If progression to the previous maximum was based on service only, ie a scale of annual increases to the maximum that is guaranteed to those who perform effectively, then this guarantee should be honoured or bought out. If progression to the old maximum was not guaranteed but was based on performance or contribution, then the new range maximum can normally be applied. Care will be needed to ensure that this does not adversely affect any specific category of staff, particularly female staff.

- Employees whose current pay is below the minimum for the new grade. Increasing pay to the minimum of the new pay range should normally be the first call on any money allocated to the assimilation process. If the total cost of rectifying underpayments is more than the organization can afford, it may be necessary to phase the necessary increases, say one portion in the current year and the rest next year. It is undesirable to phase increases over a longer period unless the circumstances are exceptional. The simplest approach is to place a maximum on the increase that any one person may receive. This can be in absolute terms (eg maximum of £2,000) or in percentage increase terms (eg maximum of 20 per cent of current pay). Another alternative is to use an annual 'gap reduction' approach (eg pay increase of 50 per cent of the difference between current pay and range minimum, or £500, whichever is the greater).

- Employees whose current pay is above the maximum for the new grade. The assimilation policy must set out how these 'red-circle' situations will be handled. The starting point is normally that no one should suffer a reduction in pay – it should be protected or safeguarded in accordance with a protection policy. Thereafter it is a matter of how quickly pay can and should be brought in line.

Protection policy

'Indefinite protection' – that is, maintaining the difference between current pay and range maximum for as long as the employee remains in the job – is highly undesirable, first because it will create permanent anomalies and, second, because, if there are a lot of men in this situation it will perpetuate unacceptable gender gaps.

Because of these considerations, the most common approach is now to protect pay for a period of between two and four years, During this time the employees will 'mark time' (ie receive no pay increases until their rate of pay falls within the new scale for their job). They will then be entitled to the same increases as any other staff in their grade up to the grade maximum. Alternatively, during the protection period, affected employees may receive a general increase/cost of living rise, but where this is the case it is less likely that an individual's pay will fall back within the new pay range during the protection period.

Where there is an incremental pay structure, staff may continue to earn increments to which they are entitled under existing arrangements up to the maximum of their present scale until the pay protection period ends, or their entitlement is bought out.

If a red-circled individual leaves the job, the scale of pay for the job reverts to the standard range as set up following job evaluation.

Implementing new grade and pay structures

Implementation can be challenging and must be planned. The steps required are:

1 Decide at the planning stage the overall change/transition strategy and timing.

2 Model the transition into the new structure and develop policies to manage this transition.

3 Develop detailed operating responsibilities and guidelines for the new structure, including the procedures for grading or regrading jobs and managing pay progression. The authority to make pay and grading decisions and methods of budgetary control should also be covered.

4 Negotiate the introduction of the new arrangements with staff representatives and trade unions, if appropriate. They should have been involved throughout the process, but the detailed 'nitty gritty' of actual pay levels and assimilation policies and procedures need to be thrashed out now.

5 Produce and distribute communications about the new structure – how it works, who will be involved in managing it and how people will be affected.

6 Design and run training workshops for managers, and possibly all staff.

7 Run a pilot or simulation exercise if feasible, operating the new approach in parts of the organization, to test its workability and robustness.

8 Full implementation and rollout. This will include giving every person information on how the new structure affects them and on their right to ask for a review of their grading if they are dissatisfied.

Tool 08
Contingent pay

Introduction

Base pay increases that are contingent on the results people achieve and their behaviour in achieving those results fall under the broad definition of performance-related or contribution-related pay. This definition emphasizes that performance is both about what has been achieved and how it has been achieved. It is in line with the views of Brumbach (1988), who wrote:

> Performance means both behaviours and results. Behaviours emanate from the performer and transform performance from abstraction to action. Not just the instruments for results, behaviours are also outcomes in their own right – the product of mental and physical effort applied to tasks – and can be judged apart from results.

Varieties of performance pay

There are three varieties of pay progression schemes that provide individuals with financial rewards in the form of increases to basic pay while varying in the criteria used to determine the level of reward:

- Performance-related pay, which is dependent on the level of results achieved.
- Competency- or competence-related pay, which is dependent on the levels of knowledge, skills or behaviour people demonstrate in carrying out their roles and is therefore a method of paying people for the ability to perform rather than what they achieve.
- Contribution-related pay, which in effect combines performance-related and competency-related pay by linking rewards to both the results achieved (outputs) and the competencies or behaviours displayed in achieving those results.

However, the distinction between these three varieties is more apparent than real. They are all concerned with performance as defined earlier. Even competency-related pay pays people for the ability to perform and it functions on the basis of assessing the level of competency people demonstrate in carrying out their roles, ie achieving results.

Purpose and contents of the tool

This tool deals with the overall approach to the development of performance pay, which is fundamentally similar for all three varieties described above. It is set out under the following headings:

- The design and development sequence;
- Analysis of context and opinions;
- Readiness for performance pay;
- Developing guiding principles;
- Setting objectives for the scheme;
- Project planning;
- Scheme design;
- Pilot testing;
- Implementing;
- Evaluating.

The design and development sequence

FIGURE 8.1 The contingent pay design and development sequence

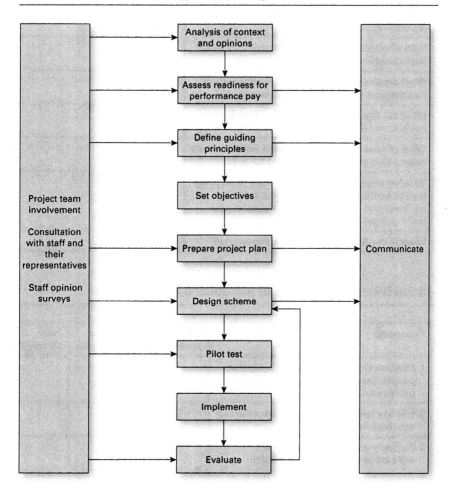

The importance of involvement and communications cannot be overestimated. Good designs will not work if these are neglected.

Analysis of context and opinions

The starting point is to review the existing context, covering what is happening now and the factors that affect contingent pay. The questionnaire set out in Figure 8.2 can be used for this purpose.

The analysis should also cover the views of line managers and employees about contingent pay by means of an opinion survey as illustrated in Figure 8.3.

FIGURE 8.2 Questionnaire: contingent pay context

Questions on the context	Answers
What are the present arrangements, if any, for contingent pay?	
How effective are any arrangements that exist? (List strengths and weaknesses.)	
What are the features of the business strategy that support the concept of contingent pay?	
What are the key behaviours that drive business performance?	
What are the main features of the organization's culture that should be taken into account?	
To what extent are employees likely to respond well to contingent pay in terms of their performance and engagement? (Analyse by main categories if appropriate.)	
What is the likely impact of contingent pay?	

FIGURE 8.3 Contingent pay opinion survey

Statement	Fully agree	Partly agree	Partly disagree	Fully disagree
1 I believe that it is right and proper that people should be rewarded for their performance.				
2 I do not believe that performance can be assessed fairly.				
3 Performance/contingent pay will encourage people to work harder.				
4 Our performance management system works well.				
5 I don't see how it is possible to measure performance accurately, fairly and consistently.				

Readiness for contingent pay

Contingent pay too often fails because the organization is not ready for it. An assessment of readiness can be made using the questionnaire shown in Figure 8.4.

FIGURE 8.4   Assessment of readiness for contingent pay

Area of readiness	Totally ready or supportive	Reasonably ready or supportive	Totally unready or unsupportive
1 There is scope for rewarding individual performance.			
2 It is believed that linking pay to performance is right for the business.			
3 It is believed by all concerned that it is right and proper to reward people according to their performance.			
4 Performance/contingent pay would both fit and support the organization's culture.			
5 Managers are capable of making fair and justifiable judgements on performance.			
6 Employees believe that current performance management processes are fair.			
7 Established performance management systems provide for expectations to be agreed and outcomes to be assessed jointly.			
8 Criteria or measures are available to assess performance.			
9 It is believed by managers and other employees that pay decisions can be fairly and equitably related to performance.			
10 It is believed that people will understand and accept the performance/contingent pay decisions that affect them.			

If the assessment is that the organization is not totally ready in any of the areas set out in Figure 8.4, consideration has to be given to why this situation exists and what can be done about it, at least to convert a totally unready assessment to a reasonably ready one. But the marked propensity for contingent pay schemes to go wrong if any of these conditions are not completely satisfied means that plans should be made on how the organization can be brought into a totally ready state, at least during the development and implementation stages.

Define guiding principles

Guiding principles need to be defined as a basis for the design and evaluation of performance or contribution pay. A questionnaire for this purpose is set out in Figure 8.5.

FIGURE 8.5 Questionnaire: contingent pay guiding principles

Possible guiding principle	Assessment of importance/ relevance: 1 vital; 2 very important; 3 fairly important; 4 not very relevant
Ensure that people are valued and rewarded fairly according to what they achieve and how they achieve it	1 2 3 4
Provide rewards for those skills and behaviours that support the future success of the individual and the organization, not just immediate past results	1 2 3 4
Deliver a clear message to staff on what the organization believes to be important in terms of performance (results) and behaviour	1 2 3 4
Adopt a fair, consistent and transparent approach to measuring and assessing performance that is based on agreed expectations and success criteria	1 2 3 4
Ensure that as far as possible judgements on performance and contribution are based on evidence, not opinion	1 2 3 4
Recognize that performance may be a function of effective team work as well as individual effort	1 2 3 4
Be developed in consultation with those concerned – managers, employees and union representatives	1 2 3 4
Be communicated to staff so that they understand the operation of the process, the part they and their managers play, and its impact on them	1 2 3 4
Devolve the maximum amount of responsibility to managers in operating the system but provide safeguards to ensure that fair and consistent decisions are made within the framework of policies and guidelines, including budgets	1 2 3 4
Provide training and guidance for managers on the system and their role in operating it	1 2 3 4
Ensure that a 'line of sight' is available so that individuals can relate the contribution they make to the reward they can attain	1 2 3 4
Provide worthwhile payments, subject to affordability	1 2 3 4
Ensure that the scheme should be controllable so that awards are made only when they have been earned	1 2 3 4

Set objectives for the scheme

Objectives should be set to provide additional guidance on the design and evaluation of performance or contribution pay. A questionnaire for this purpose is set out in Figure 8.6.

FIGURE 8.6 Questionnaire: contingent pay objectives

Possible objectives	Assessment of importance/ relevance: 1 vital; 2 very important; 3 fairly important; 4 not very relevant
Recognize and reward better performance	1 2 3 4
Deliver a message about the importance of performance	1 2 3 4
Improve organizational performance	1 2 3 4
Attract and retain high-quality people	1 2 3 4
Increase employee engagement	1 2 3 4
Support cultural change	1 2 3 4
Focus attention on key results and values	1 2 3 4
Other	

Project planning

The design and implementation of a contingent pay scheme is a much more demanding and time-consuming process than most people appreciate. The success of the scheme depends on the thoroughness with which it has been prepared and the care taken in putting it into effect. It is particularly important to appreciate that equal if not more attention has to be paid to getting the process of operating the scheme right as to designing its basic features. A carefully planned and managed project is required. The normal rules of project management apply.

Project planning involves setting up a project team, deciding on the sequence and timing of activities and establishing the resources required (people and money). The activities will include design and implementation planning and developing and actioning a communications strategy.

Project planning should not only ensure that the right things get done on time and within budget but also that procedures and systems are set up for monitoring and evaluating the outcomes.

Design scheme

The design steps involve decisions on:

- the scope for pay progression;
- how pay progression should be controlled;
- how performance should be assessed;
- the use of rating or narrative summaries of assessments;
- methods of converting assessments to pay if rating is used;
- methods of converting assessments to pay if narrative assessments are used;
- timing of performance pay reviews.

Scope for pay progression

A decision has to be made on the scope for pay progression provided by the width or span of the pay ranges in a graded pay structure or zones in a broad-banded structure. The 2004 e-reward survey of pay structures established that the most common width measured by the size of the pay span as a percentage of the lower limit of the range was between 50 and 59 per cent, which is typical in a broad-graded structure (18 per cent of respondents). But 15 per cent of respondents had widths of between 30 and 39 per cent, which is typical in a narrow-graded structure.

Control of pay progression

Pay progression within ranges must be controlled. The methods available are:

- Threshold control: a point is defined in the pay range beyond which pay cannot increase unless individuals achieve a defined level of achievement or competence.
- Segment or zone control: an extension of threshold control, which involves dividing the grade into a number, often three, segments or zones.
- Reference point control: scope is provided for progression according to competence by increments to the reference point. Thereafter, individuals may earn cash bonuses for high achievement, that may be consolidated up to the maximum pay for the grade if high achievement levels are sustained.

Assessment of performance

The methods used to assess performance should be based on:

- an effective performance management system; use the questionnaire in Figure 8.7;
- an effective process for goal setting as a basis for measuring results; use the questionnaire in Figure 8.8;
- an effective process for measuring levels of performance in terms of results (for a traditional performance-related pay scheme or a contribution-related pay scheme); use the questionnaire in Figure 8.9;
- an effective process for measuring levels of competency if competency is used as a criterion (in a competency-related or contribution-related scheme); use the questionnaire in Figure 8.10;
- a fair and transparent process for recording judgements about performance by a rating system or other means; use the criteria in Figure 8.11.

FIGURE 8.7 Questionnaire: performance management system

Rate the following statements on a scale of 1–5 where: 1 = fully agree, 2 = agree, 3 = not sure, 4 = disagree, 5 = strongly disagree	
Our performance management system:	
1 Translates corporate goals into divisional, departmental, team and individual goals.	1 2 3 4 5
2 Helps to clarify corporate goals.	1 2 3 4 5
3 Is a continuous and evolutionary process in which performance improves over time.	1 2 3 4 5
4 Relies on consensus and cooperation rather than control and coercion.	1 2 3 4 5
5 Creates a shared understanding of what is required to improve performance and how it will be achieved.	1 2 3 4 5
6 Encourages self-management of individual performance.	1 2 3 4 5
7 Encourages a management style that is open and honest and encourages two-way communication between managers and staff at all levels.	1 2 3 4 5
8 Delivers continuous feedback on organizational, team and individual performance to all staff.	1 2 3 4 5
9 Analyses and assesses performance against jointly agreed goals.	1 2 3 4 5
10 Enables individual staff members to modify their objectives.	1 2 3 4 5
11 Demonstrates respect for the individual.	1 2 3 4 5
12 Has fair procedures.	1 2 3 4 5

FIGURE 8.8   Questionnaire: goal setting

Rate the following statements on a scale of 1–5 where: 1 = fully agree, 2 = agree, 3 = not sure, 4 = disagree, 5 = strongly disagree	
1 The goal-setting process is generally based on an agreed and up-to-date role profile that sets out key result areas.	1 2 3 4 5
2 Goals clearly relate to key result areas in the role profile.	1 2 3 4 5
3 If goals have been cascaded downwards, there is some scope for individuals to discuss and modify their own goals.	1 2 3 4 5
4 Goal setting is always carried out jointly by the manager and the individual.	1 2 3 4 5
5 Individual goals generally provide clear and specific support to the achievement of team and department goals.	1 2 3 4 5
6 Goals are generally specific and time related.	1 2 3 4 5
7 Goals are generally challenging.	1 2 3 4 5
8 Goals are generally realistic and attainable.	1 2 3 4 5
9 Success criteria for each goal are usually determined.	1 2 3 4 5
10 The goal-setting and agreement process provides a realistic and objective basis for assessing performance.	1 2 3 4 5

FIGURE 8.9   Questionnaire: results assessment

Rate the following statements on a scale of 1–5 where: 1 = fully agree, 2 = agree, 3 = not sure, 4 = disagree, 5 = strongly disagree	
1 Objectives are generally agreed between managers and their staff.	1 2 3 4 5
2 Fair and consistent methods are used to measure results against objectives.	1 2 3 4 5
3 Managers have been thoroughly trained in agreeing objectives and assessing results.	1 2 3 4 5
4 Assessments provide a reliable guide to decisions on performance pay.	1 2 3 4 5
5 Staff feel that the methods used to assess results are fair.	1 2 3 4 5

Use of ratings or narrative assessments

The most typical approach is to convert assessments into ratings. Alternatively, narrative assessments can be used. The advantages and disadvantages of each approach are summarized in Figure 8.11.

If rating is preferred to overall narrative assessments, then the following decisions will need to be made:

FIGURE 8.10   Questionnaire: competency assessment

Rate the following statements on a scale of 1–5 where: *1 = fully agree, 2 = agree, 3 = not sure, 4 = disagree, 5 = strongly disagree*	
1 A well researched, clear and realistic competency framework provides a basis for assessing levels of competency.	1 2 3 4 5
2 Criterion referencing (comparing one measure unit a criterion in the form of another measure) has been used to analyse the key aspects of behaviour that differentiate between effective and less effective performance.	1 2 3 4 5
3 Clear definitions of acceptable and unacceptable behaviour exist for each competency areas based on criterion referencing.	1 2 3 4 5
4 The definitions of acceptable and unacceptable behaviour provide useful guidance on assessments.	1 2 3 4 5
5 Managers have been thoroughly trained in interpreting the competency framework and definitions.	1 2 3 4 5
6 Managers are able to agree competency requirements with their staff.	1 2 3 4 5
7 Managers are able to assess levels of competency by reference to the competency framework and the behaviour of their staff.	1 2 3 4 5
8 Competency assessments provide a useful guide to decisions on contribution pay.	1 2 3 4 5
9 Staff feel that the methods used to assess competency are fair.	1 2 3 4 5
10 It is possible to relate competency assessments to individual performance levels.	1 2 3 4 5

- How ratings will be made for results, or for results and level of competence. In the latter case, two ratings may be required.
- The number of levels required – four or five are the most typical.
- How each level should be defined – this should provide as much guidance as possible to the manager making the assessment.
- How managers should be trained in rating – this is vital and can take the form of workshops in which managers carry out simulated ratings and jointly analyse the rationale for their decisions, so that they gain a better understanding of what the rating levels mean by reference to realistic examples.
- The steps that can be taken to monitor ratings to ensure that they are reasonably fair and consistent.
- The methods that can be used to guide rating decisions – broad guidelines at one extreme; forced distribution at the other.
- The methods that can be used to achieve consistency, such as HR monitoring, peer review, calibration workshops or focused training.

FIGURE 8.11   Arguments for and against ratings and narrative assessments

Ratings		Narrative assessments	
Arguments for	**Arguments against**	**Arguments for**	**Arguments against**
They provide a clear basis for making performance pay decisions. They let people know where they stand. It is necessary to sum up judgments about people.	Ratings are likely to be subjective and inconsistent. Line managers tend not to differentiate between ratings. The use of ratings to inform decisions on performance pay will dominate performance reviews and prejudice the real purpose of such reviews, ie to provide the basis for developing skills and improving performance.	Gets rid of the negative associations of ratings.	Does not provide a clear basis for performance pay decisions. May be vague and inconclusive.

If the decision is not to have rating, then it will be necessary to provide guidelines on how narrative assessments should be made. These can suggest that:

- The narrative should be based on a systematic assessment of performance or competence under the headings set out in a performance agreement or against the key result areas in a role profile.
- Any judgements made should be supported by evidence.
- An overall summary should be supported by reference to the evidence.
- The individual concerned should be given the opportunity to take part in making the assessment and should see and be able to comment on the final assessment.

It is essential to train managers in making narrative assessments using simulations and examples.

Converting ratings into pay decisions

The most typical approach, especially in traditional performance-related pay schemes, is to have a single rating based on performance in achieving results. An alternative approach, often referred to as contribution-related pay, is to have two ratings, one for results (outputs) and the other for competency level (inputs), or a combined rating can be used.

FIGURE 8.12 Simple link between results rating and pay increase

Rating	% increase
A	6
B	4
C	3
D	2
E	0

FIGURE 8.13 A pay matrix

Rating	Percentage pay increase according to performance rating and position in pay range (compa-ratio)			
	Position in pay range			
	80%–90%	*91%–100%*	*101%–110%*	*111%–120%*
Excellent	12%	10%	8%	6%
Very effective	10%	8%	6%	4%
Effective	6%	4%	3%	0
Developing	4%	3%	0	0
Ineligible	0	0	0	0

Results rating

The simplest method is to have a direct link between a results rating and the pay increase, as shown for example in Figure 8.12.

A more sophisticated approach is to use a pay matrix as illustrated in Figure 8.13. This indicates the percentage increase payable for different performance ratings according to the position of the individual's pay in the pay range. This is sometimes referred to as an individual 'compa-ratio' and expresses pay as a percentage of the mid point in a range. A compa-ratio of 100 per cent means that the salary would be at the mid point.

Ratings of both results and competency levels

Rating both results and competency levels can be carried out using the matrix shown in Figure 8.14.

FIGURE 8.14 A results and competency contribution pay matrix

	Percentage pay increase according to performance rating and competence assessment		
Results rating	**Competency assessment**		
	Developing – does not yet meet all competence standards	**Fully competent – meets all competence standards**	**Highly competent – exceeds most competence standards**
Exceptional	–	8%	10%
Very effective	–	6%	7%
Effective	–	4%	5%
Developing	3%	–	–
Ineligible	0	–	–

Converting assessments into pay decisions if narratives are used

A framework for narrative assessments is illustrated in Figure 8.15.

If a narrative assessment is used, it is still necessary to convert it into a decision on the level of performance pay increase that should be awarded. If pay reviews are conducted separately from performance reviews (which is desirable), narrative assessments can be converted into pay increases simply by making a judgement on the level of increase that should be awarded, taking all aspects of performance into account: for example, exceptional, above average, average, below average or nil. The pay increase dimensions attached to these judgements (for example: exceptional 8 per cent; above average 5 per cent; average 3 per cent; below average 2 per cent), could be decided by management when setting pay review policy. Reviewing managers could be informed of what is regarded as a reasonable distribution of these awards, say 5 per cent, 15 per cent, 60 per cent and 15 per cent with 5 per cent ineligible. These could be treated as broad guidelines, or a forced distribution approach could be adopted, which means that they would be mandatory.

Timing of performance pay reviews

A policy decision is required as to whether or not the performance and pay reviews should be decoupled, ie held on separate dates. Decoupling means that the performance review can focus on performance and development issues and not be diverted by pay considerations. Of course, there has to be a 'read-across' from the performance to the reward review but the latter can simply involve making recommendations on the levels of pay increases, taking into account the assessment of performance or contribution but also how well individuals are paid in relation to their peers who are performing at similar levels.

FIGURE 8.15   Narrative assessment

Reviewer rating based on assessment of achievement against job requirements, objectives and applied skills and knowledge	
Description	Tick description that best fits; comment if appropriate
Exceptional: has demonstrated outstanding contribution in the job through a combination of exceptional achievement against objectives and job requirements: is recognized by others as a role model in their job, both with respect to what they have done and how they have gone about doing it.	
Value added: has demonstrated a positive contribution that adds sustained value, through achievements in the job and how the individual has done it, demonstrating growth and development in the job.	
Acceptable: undertaking the job to a satisfactory level; getting on with the job to a level that is regarded as satisfactory; generally meets objectives without adding sustained additional value over the course of the year.	
Under-performing: performance in the job has not met required standards (it is expected that performance management steps will already have been taken to deal with performance issues).	

The other decisions required for an individual pay review are:

- the total budget available, eg 3 per cent of payroll;
- the distribution of increases in accordance with ratings or assessments to fit the budget;
- whether an equal pay review or regular auditing indicates that any anomalies need to be addressed, eg as a result of high recruitment salaries;
- the instructions to be issued to managers on conducting the review – their budgets and the distribution of awards as guidelines or as a forced distribution;
- the methods to be used for monitoring review decisions to ensure that the budget is not exceeded and the guidelines are followed.

Conduct pilot scheme

Contingent pay schemes can look good on paper but, too often, they work badly in practice. It is therefore helpful to conduct a pilot test. This could be in the form of a 'dummy run' in which the scheme is run in two or three representative departments. In smaller organizations the first year of implementation may be treated as a trial run. In both cases this would involve going through each stage of the process but not using the outcomes to generate pay increases. Managers and their staff will have to be carefully briefed on the purpose of the test and persuaded that it is in everyone's interest, including their own, that the test should take place.

The aims would be to test:

- the format and effectiveness of budgets and guidelines;
- the utility of the information given to managers to help them in decision making;
- the effectiveness of the training given to managers;
- the quality of the ratings and assessments made;
- the effectiveness of the procedures used, including records of recommendations and decision records;

FIGURE 8.16   Pilot scheme opinion survey: managers

Rate the following statements on a scale of 1–5 where: *1 = fully agree, 2 = agree, 3 = not sure, 4 = disagree, 5 = strongly disagree*	
1 As a whole, the scheme worked very well.	1 2 3 4 5
2 The training I was given was very useful.	1 2 3 4 5
3 The guidelines were helpful.	1 2 3 4 5
4 The scheme should help to improve performance.	1 2 3 4 5
5 I found it difficult to make assessments.	1 2 3 4 5
6 The scheme should be introduced as it stands.	1 2 3 4 5
Other comments and suggestions	

FIGURE 8.17   Pilot scheme opinion survey: employees

Rate the following statements on a scale of 1–5 where: *1 = fully agree, 2 = agree, 3 = not sure, 4 = disagree, 5 = strongly disagree*	
1 As a whole, the scheme worked very well.	1 2 3 4 5
2 The assessment and recommendation by my manager were fair.	1 2 3 4 5
3 The proposed increase to my pay was reasonable.	1 2 3 4 5
4 I fully understood how my increase in pay was/will be decided.	1 2 3 4 5
5 The scheme will encourage me to improve my performance.	1 2 3 4 5
6 The scheme should be introduced as it stands.	1 2 3 4 5
Other comments and suggestions	

- the methods of controlling the review by reference to budgets and guidelines;
- importantly, the reactions of reviewing managers and their staff to the process.

On the last point above, Figures 8.16 and 8.17 show examples of survey questionnaires that can be used to obtain these reactions.

Implement scheme

The implementation plan should cover:

- how it will be introduced smoothly;
- how details of the scheme will be communicated to line managers, employees generally and their representatives;
- how managers will be briefed and trained;
- how the effectiveness of the scheme will be monitored and evaluated.

Evaluate scheme

The evaluation process should cover:

- the extent to which the scheme's objectives have been attained;
- how well the scheme has operated;
- the reactions of managers and employees to the scheme;
- a review of the scheme to identify and eliminate any gender discrimination.

Attainment of objectives

A framework for evaluating the achievement of the scheme's objectives is given in Figure 8.18.

In addition, the reactions of managers and other employees to the scheme can be established through using the questionnaires in Figures 8.16 and 8.17 again.

Reviewing the performance pay scheme for gender discrimination

To eliminate or at least reduce the risk of gender discrimination the checklist in Figure 8.19 should be completed. If the answer is no to any of these questions, it will be necessary to investigate the practice to ensure it is free from sex discrimination.

FIGURE 8.18 Framework for evaluating attainment of objectives

Objective	Success criteria	Evaluation

FIGURE 8.19 Checklist: gender discrimination

	Yes	No
1 Are women and men equally entitled to participate in performance/contribution pay?		
2 If so, are the outcomes proportionate?		
3 Are part-time workers or those on fixed, short-term, term-time or indefinite contracts equally entitled to participate in performance/contribution pay?		
4 If so, are the outcomes proportionate?		
5 Are unbiased criteria used to assess eligibility for merit pay or accelerated/additional increments?		
6 Are performance ratings and pay awards checked regularly to identify any examples of bias?		
7 Is there any evidence of bias in the distribution of performance ratings?		
8 Is there any evidence of bias in the award of performance/contribution pay?		
9 If there are any differences in performance/contribution, can they be objectively justified?		
10 Have those responsible for making decisions on performance/contribution pay been appropriately trained in best employment practice based on equality and diversity legislation?		

Reference

Brumbach, G B (1988) Some ideas, issues and predictions about performance management, *Public Personnel Management*, winter, pp 387–402

Tool 09
Bonus schemes

Introduction

Bonus schemes provide cash payments to employees that are related to the performance of the organization, team or individuals, or a combination of two or more of these. Bonuses are often referred to as 'variable pay' or 'pay-at-risk'.

A defining characteristic of a bonus is that it has to be re-earned, unlike increases that are consolidated into base pay and arise from individual contingent pay schemes such as performance- or contribution-related pay or pay related to service. Cash bonuses may be the sole method of providing people with rewards in addition to their base pay, or they may be paid on top of individual contingent pay. Bonus schemes are a popular method of reward. The 2009 CIPD reward survey reported that 71 per cent of the 729 participating companies apply some form of variable pay scheme. IRS 2009 research put the figure at 80 per cent.

The aims of bonus schemes may differ, but typically they include one or more of the following characteristics:

- enhance the performance–reward connection;
- enable people to share in the success of the organization and therefore increase their commitment and sense of identity;
- provide rewards related to business performance, to increase motivation, commitment and engagement;
- provide a direct incentive to increase motivation and generate higher future levels of individual and team performance;
- ensure that pay levels are competitive and will attract and retain good-quality people;
- provide flexibility to the organization's remuneration policy by rewarding employees for good performance without permanently increasing the pay bill.

Well managed and designed, bonus schemes can encourage employees to focus on the key value drivers for an organization, motivate people to succeed and ensure that pay is competitive, while at the same time allowing everyone to share in the success of the business. Badly administered and designed, they can demotivate employees and prove an expensive indulgence of little strategic and organizational value. Or put another way, 'variable pay can float like a butterfly, sting like a bee' (Schuster and Zingheim, 2000). An IRS 2009 survey reported that 75 per cent of employers said that their bonus schemes were effective in meeting their stated objectives. However, only just over half of respondents agreed that bonus schemes have a positive impact on company performance, which raises questions about whether bonus schemes always provide an effective return on investment.

Purpose of the tool

The purpose of this tool is to provide practical guidance to any organization that wants to develop and introduce new bonus schemes, review existing schemes, maintain their effectiveness and evaluate their impact. The tool contains:

- A general introduction in which bonus schemes are defined and their aims and features described, including a description of the purpose and features of major types of bonus schemes;
- A description of the five stages involved in developing, managing and reviewing bonus schemes.

Schemes defined

This tool covers bonus schemes that generate cash awards contingent on individual, team or organization performance. Schemes can be classified into seven broad categories. Figure 9.1 summarizes the main features and advantages and risks of the different types of scheme.

Developing a bonus scheme

Developing an effective bonus scheme requires great care and a disciplined methodology. The success or failure of schemes depends as much on the way in which the bonus plan is developed, implemented and operated as on its design.

This tool describes a five-step process for developing and implementing a bonus scheme (Figure 9.2). These steps can be added to and adjusted to

FIGURE 9.1 Features, advantages and risks of different bonus schemes

Type of scheme	Main features	Advantages	Risks
Profit sharing	Payment of sums in cash related to the profits of the business. Such schemes operate on corporate basis and usually make profit shares available to all employees except possibly directors or senior managers.	Increases identification with the organization. Recognizes that everyone contributes to creating profit.	Does not provide an individual incentive. Amounts distributed are taken for granted.
Business performance schemes	Payments related to performance of whole business or a major function such as a division, store or site. Performance measured by key performance indicators (KPIs) – eg profit, contribution, shareholder value, earnings per share or economic value added.	Enables employees to share in organization's success thus increasing commitment. Can focus on range of key factors affecting organizational performance. Can readily be added to other forms of contingent pay to recognize collective as distinct from individual effort.	Does not provide an individual incentive. It may be difficult for some employees to see 'line of sight' between their own performance and business performance.
Team pay	Payments to members of a formally established team are linked to performance of that team. Rewards shared among members of team in accordance with published formula or on ad hoc basis in case of exceptional achievements.	Encourages team working. Enhances flexible working and multi-skilling. Clarifies team goals. Encourages less effective performers to improve by meeting team standards.	May be difficult to identify well defined teams with clear and measurable goals. Individuals may resent fact their own performance is not recognized. Risk of 'free-loaders' if individual performance is not effectively managed.

FIGURE 9.1 *Continued*

Type of scheme	Main features	Advantages	Risks
Gainsharing	Formula-based company or factory-wide bonus plan which provides for employees to share in the financial gains made by a company as a result of its improved performance as measured, for example, by added value. In some schemes the formula also incorporates performance measures relating to quality, customer service, delivery or cost reduction.	Recognizes that everyone working in a plant contributes to creating added value and should benefit accordingly. Provides a platform for the joint analysis of methods of improving productivity.	Does not provide an individual incentive. Can be complex. Ineffective if too high a proportion of added value is retained by the company.
Individual bonus or incentive plans	Payments related to individual performance. May be related to performance assessment through annual appraisal. Payments typically linked to achievement of objectives. Levels of award may be restricted to certain categories of staff (more common for management) and vary by level in organization, with higher bonus potential typically available for higher levels of management or sales staff on grounds that these can more directly affect performance of the organization.	Provides direct reward related to specific achievements and future targets, constituting both a reward and an incentive. Cash, if sufficiently high, can make an immediate impact on motivation and engagement. Lump sum payments appeal to some people. Additional rewards can be given to people at the top of their base pay range without damaging the integrity of the pay structure.	Some people may prefer consolidated increases to base pay rather than rely on possibly unpredictable bonus payments that may be perceived as arbitrary, and which are likely to be non-pensionable. They can be more difficult to apply to people whose jobs have less tangible outputs. People may be diverted from the innovative and developmental aspects of their work due to focusing on the job in hand. It might be hard to discriminate fairly between those on long-term projects and those with shorter-term and more visible outputs. It can be difficult to guarantee consistency of objective setting and performance review. Does not reinforce collaborative behaviours.

FIGURE 9.1 *Continued*

Type of scheme	Main features	Advantages	Risks
Combination plans	Payments related to a combination of plans measuring performance across any combination of corporate, team and/or individual performance.	Combines advantages of different types of bonus arrangements – eg business and individual (most common form of combination scheme).	May be over-complex. Could disperse impact of either collective or individual elements.
Project and ad hoc bonuses	Award schemes or one-off awards paid out for specific achievements or success.	Schemes can be devolved to line management and paid out more spontaneously than payments made under annual bonus schemes. May require less formal approval process.	Does not directly motivate employees to perform better because awards are ad hoc. Requires central monitoring to ensure consistency of approach across different parts of the organization.

FIGURE 9.2   Stages in the introduction and management of a bonus scheme

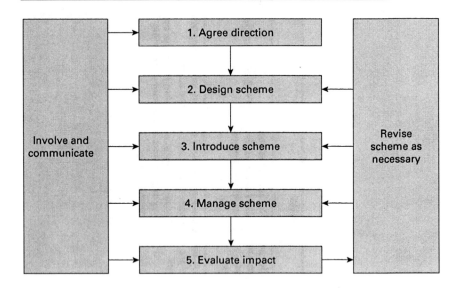

the organization's culture, objectives and specific needs. Depending on the circumstances, the steps need not be followed sequentially; however any development or redesign of a bonus scheme should incorporate all aspects of the design process.

Stage 1: Agree direction

This is the preliminary stage when the notion of a bonus scheme is being considered and initial ideas on the scheme are explored. The key points that need to be covered are:

- the rationale for introducing or amending a scheme;
- choosing a scheme;
- who will be covered by the scheme and why;
- developing the business case;
- involvement and communications.

Rationale

In practice many organizations start from an assumption that variable pay is desirable (or not) and then develop pay arrangements to support this assumption. Instead, the flowchart in Figure 9.3 assumes that the starting point should be understanding what success means in the organization,

FIGURE 9.3 Flowchart: rationale for variable pay

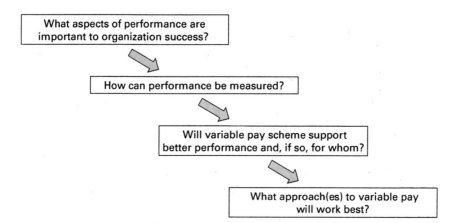

what aspects of performance underpin this and what aspects of performance are measurable. Only then is a decision made about whether and how variable pay is likely to support this performance.

Whether or not a bonus scheme is appropriate will depend on a combination of factors including organization culture, ability to manage performance effectively and competitive practice. The rationale for a bonus scheme, and the decision on what type of scheme would be appropriate can be considered in the context of the organizational priorities set out in Figure 9.4 and the interview guide in Figure 9.5.

The results of this analysis may or may not result in the conclusion that one or more types of bonus scheme are appropriate. If so, consideration should be given not only to scheme design, but also to whether the bonus scheme will be an alternative to or supplement contingent base pay arrangements. The advantages and disadvantages of these two approaches are summarized in Figure 9.6.

Choosing a scheme

The decision grid in Figure 9.7 provides a diagnostic tool that can be used to trigger discussion about what type of scheme may be appropriate. The horizontal axis focuses on whether bonus arrangements are intended to act as a financial incentive to drive future behaviour and actions, or as a 'thank you' and recognition of past performance. The vertical axis takes into account whether the bonus arrangements are aimed at individual performance or collective performance (ranging on a scale through individual, team, department, division/subsidiary to corporate level). Thus a profit-sharing scheme would be plotted at the top left hand corner of the grid, whereas a sales commission plan based solely on individual performance would feature in the bottom right hand corner.

FIGURE 9.4 Prioritizing pay objectives

What are our priorities?	Importance ranking (1 to 5)	What this means for our pay system
Provide an incentive to perform well		
Ensure that total cash levels are competitive		
Help attract and retain staff		
Communicate organizational strategic goals		
Support changing culture/values		
Reinforce key business objectives		
Let employees share in the success of the business		
Reflect what our competitors are doing		
Reinforce key behaviours/standards		
Help improve individual performance		
Help create a link between employee and organizational performance		
Motivate staff by establishing a clear link between pay and performance		
Reward one-off achievements		
Help contain wage costs		
Reinforce team cohesiveness		

FIGURE 9.5 Variable pay interview guide

Variable pay intentions: interview guide
Who delivers critical performance with respect to our business goals?
To what extent does the organization want to differentiate itself through its pay arrangements?
What is more important: recognition of the whole organization's contribution over the past year or incentivizing future performance through rewarding individual examples of outstanding achievement – or both?
Does the organization have a clear view about whether or not to communicate and recognize organization-wide goals and achievements through pay?
Does the organization want a mechanism to keep base pay costs down by limiting base pay increases and placing more emphasis on variable pay?
Is the organization committed to leveraging performance through pay?

FIGURE 9.5 *Continued*

Variable pay intentions: interview guide
Is there evidence that the organization will be better able to recruit and retain staff if there is a bonus scheme?
What is more important to employees: risk sharing or security of income?
Has the organization currently got the balance right between base pay and lump sum awards (if applicable)?
Are there any issues about reputational risk management for the organization in being seen to make 'bonus' awards?
What proportion of staff in the organization are genuinely high or outstanding performers? Does the organization want to reward only exceptional performance or targeted achievement?
Do you want pay arrangements to be applied equally to all staff, top to bottom – or should there be any differentiation by level?/type of role?
What approach to pay is most cost effective for the organization and likely to provide the best return on investment?
To what extent should the pay system be self-financing?
Does management have the skill to manage a performance/pay relationship effectively?

FIGURE 9.6 The relationship between bonus/contingent pay arrangements

Approach	Advantages	Disadvantages
Bonus only	Has to be re-earned. Can be related to corporate or team performance as well as individual performance, thereby increasing commitment and enhancing teamwork. Cash sums, as long as they are sizeable, can have more immediate impact on motivation and engagement.	May be perceived as arbitrary. May not be pensionable. Some people may prefer opportunity to increase their base pay rather than rely on potentially unpredictable bonus payments.
Bonus and contingent pay	Get the best of both worlds – consolidated increases and cash payments.	Potentially complex. Impact made by either bonuses or consolidated payments might be dissipated, especially when sums available are divided into two parts.

FIGURE 9.7 Diagnostic tool – bonus options

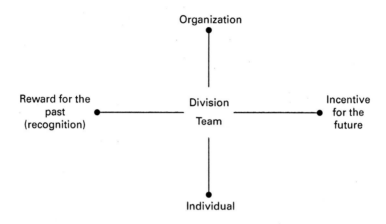

Figure 9.8 provides another tool for analysing the relative importance of rewarding corporate, team and individual performance, taking into account conditions for success and the current organizational environment. Scheme options can also be plotted on a decision grid. Figure 9.9 can be used to plot which scheme is most likely to meet different objectives, with the vertical access being amended as appropriate to reflect organizational objectives.

When all the options have been reviewed it should be possible to plot how each aspect of performance relates to an individual's pay. Figure 9.10 shows an example of one organization that has decided to reward ongoing value with base pay and results with a range of bonuses.

Eligibility

Having decided that a bonus scheme is appropriate, a decision is needed on who will be covered by the scheme. Typical issues relating to eligibility under the various types of scheme can be summarized as follows:

- Bonus schemes based on *individual performance* may be limited to managers on the grounds that they make the greatest impact on results and should be incentivized and rewarded for their contribution to those results. But this may frustrate other staff who, with justification, could argue that they also make a contribution that deserves a reward.

- Bonuses based on *business performance* may be provided for all staff, or for subdivisions of the business or teams. This may raise issues of equity if a scheme is applied in one part of the organization and not another.

- *Profit sharing* usually applies to all staff, although directors may be excluded and rewarded with bonuses. Also, employees covered by other bonus schemes (eg a business-unit performance or gainsharing

FIGURE 9.8 Prioritizing corporate, team and individual performance

Purpose/objectives	Importance *very important* *quite important* *marginal*	Impact *significant* *moderate* *negligible*	Critical success factors	Current status *good* *satisfactory* *poor*
Corporate Creating a sense of sharing in corporate success Building overall team work and identity Creating some flexibility in total payroll costs Improving communications on organizational performance			Clear organizational mission One or more measures that sum up overall corporate performance Confidence in the measurement of performance Good communications systems	
Team Creating a sense of team work Increasing the sense of fairness about rewards by basing them on team results Improving team performance Creating some flexibility in total pay costs Improving communications on how the team/unit can contribute to improved corporate results			Clearly established, stable teams Measures that sum up team performance and meet corporate needs Confidence in the measurement of performance A review process to ensure consistency of approach (cross-organizational)	
Individual To focus energy and attention on key tasks To ensure performance management is treated seriously Increasing the sense of fairness about rewards Creating flexibility in total pay costs			Clear individual objectives Processes for ensuring dialogue between individuals Targets which are perceived as fair Skills of managers in setting objectives, monitoring and measuring performance Review processes to ensure consistency	

FIGURE 9.9   Decision grid: bonus options

	Achievement of individual targets	Operating team results	Reinforce key behaviours	Organization profitability/key performance measure(s)	Special achievements	Individual productivity	Ease/cost of implementation
Base pay							
Individual bonus							
Team bonus							
Gainsharing							
Business performance							
Profit share							
Spot awards							
Ad hoc awards							

FIGURE 9.10   Clarifying the relationship between performance elements and reward

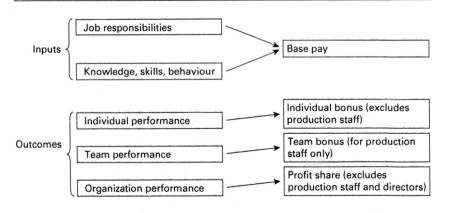

scheme) may not participate, particularly if that scheme has potential to yield higher reward (and possibly higher risk) than the profit-share arrangements.

- *Gainsharing* is usually provided for employees in a particular plant where costs and performance improvements can be clearly measured. Participation may be restricted to manual workers.

FIGURE 9.11 Checklist: the business rationale

- What approach is being advocated and why?
- Why has this approach been proposed for a particular category or categories of staff?
- What impact will a bonus scheme for a particular category or categories of staff make on organizational, team or individual performance?
- How will it make that impact?
- If we already have a performance- or contribution-related pay scheme, why is a bonus scheme necessary?
- If we do not have a performance- or contribution-related pay scheme, why is a bonus scheme preferable?
- How much will the investment in a bonus scheme cost in terms of the cost of developing it and the cost of the bonus payments?
- Will it be self-financing?
- Does the return on that investment in terms of the impact on performance justify a scheme?

- *Ad hoc/project bonuses* are often available for all categories of staff, excluding senior management. They can be made either to individuals or to teams.

- *Combination plans* may be applied to all staff, although the performance measures and payment formula may vary for different levels/categories of staff, as they are sometimes restricted to managers.

Developing the business case

If the questions about overall direction, scheme type and eligibility can be answered, a business case can be developed that addresses the questions in Figure 9.11. This involves not only confirming what type of scheme is appropriate, but assumptions about scheme funding and return on investment.

Involvement and communications

Employee involvement may start when the dialogue about reward direction is initiated. However, if it hasn't started by the time the business case has been developed it is advisable to begin consultation before embarking on the process of detailed scheme design. The importance of involving employees and communicating to them the purpose and details of the scheme cannot be overestimated. It is essential to involve those who will be affected in considering the options and designing the scheme. It is equally important to let those people know what is being proposed, why it is being proposed and how it will affect them. It is also necessary to ensure that the scheme's business rationale is understood and accepted as it will be used as a point of reference in evaluating the scheme (Stage 5 below).

Stage 2: Design scheme

There is no such thing as a standard bonus scheme. They all have to be individually tailored to meets the needs of the organization and the circumstances in which bonuses will be earned. However, all scheme designs should cover the same main features, including:

- Purpose: the scheme's objectives;
- Eligibility: to whom the scheme will apply;
- Performance criteria: the performance measures and method of assessment;
- Bonus potential: amount of bonus to be distributed according to different levels of performance, including caps on awards;
- Method of distributing payments: how payment is expressed (eg as a percentage of salary or a cash amount) and frequency;
- Scheme funding: how the scheme will be funded in order to provide meaningful rewards to the staff affected;
- Ensuring that the costs of the scheme are modelled – using a range of different business scenarios;
- Scheme administration: policy guidance on scheme governance.

Determining the performance criteria and formula for payment can be the most challenging part of scheme design. The bonus formula establishes the relationship between the performance factors used in the plan and the reward. It also fixes the size of the bonus pool or fund to be distributed to those eligible for the bonus, or the scale of payments made to employees in relation to performance with regard to certain criteria.

Figure 9.12 provides a checklist of what to address in developing the performance formula.

FIGURE 9.12 Checklist: bonus formula

Question	Issues
What performance criteria will be used?	The measures used must be important, meaningful to participants and measurable. Beware of selecting performance criteria that are easiest to measure rather than the most important.
	Avoid using too many measures, as this dilutes the performance message.
	Is the outcome the end product of a course of events that the individual, team or business unit can actually influence?
	Can performance standards/measures be manipulated by the participants?
	Are the goals compatible with and coordinated with results expected from other individuals/ different areas of the organization?
	Are the goals supportive of long-term success rather than just short term?
How will performance criteria be measured, eg: • an absolute standard of performance? • performance relative to previous years? • performance relative to competitors?	Each type of measure has benefits and risks. These need to be fully evaluated.
What is the performance threshold for bonus payments?	What is the performance bar beneath which no bonus will be payable? And is there an upper limit of performance beyond which no further bonus is payable?
To what extent should individual performance impact on payments under a team, business performance or profit share scheme?	Should individual performance be used to modify payments, eg in the event of underperformance?
Combined plans only: what is the split between corporate, department, team and individual bonus element?	To what extent might this need to vary depending on the level of employee or which part of the organization they work in?
Are performance measures to be weighted?	Where there is a range of performance measures, will a formula be applied to weight them?

The potential size of bonus payments and how bonus awards are calculated are a matter of judgement. But to be effective, bonuses not only have to be achievable, but also worth having. The amount should be related to:

- the size of bonus that is deemed sufficient to provide an adequate incentive or reward to motivate eligible employees;
- the importance generally attached to financial rewards by the organization and its employees;
- policy on the proportion of total remuneration that it is believed should be at risk;
- whether bonus is effectively deferred earnings for achieving targets or whether it is intended to play a significant role in driving behaviour and activities;
- what the organization believes it can afford to pay – to what extent is the scheme expected to be self-financing?

With respect to the method of bonus calculation, Figure 9.13 provides a checklist of issues to consider.

FIGURE 9.13   Checklist: bonus calculation

- Should bonus increase linearly with performance or should the slope of the bonus/performance payment vary with level of performance reflecting the relative difficulty of achieving bonus?
- Is there a case for deferring some part of the bonus award to aid employee retention or to protect the employer by ensuring that the scheme does not focus solely on short-term performance? (This is only likely to be feasible where bonuses are a significant proportion of earnings.)
- How will bonuses be distributed, eg as a percentage of actual pay, a percentage of grade/level mid point or as a cash amount?
- If bonuses are linked to actual pay, is bonus to be based on year-end salary or averaged for the performance period?
- How often will bonuses be paid – for example, monthly, quarterly or annually – and how does this relate to the business planning cycle?
- How often will the bonus formula be reviewed?
- How do the bonus calculations relate to overall bonus funding – using different business scenarios will the bonus scheme be affordable?

Stage 3: Introduce scheme

The successful introduction of a bonus scheme is dependent on thorough testing and preparation. Figure 9.14 provides an implementation checklist.

FIGURE 9.14   Implementation checklist

Implementation checklist: have you:	Yes	No
Modelled potential out-turns based on actual past performance or future business scenarios and drawn up a budget for the scheme to ensure that it is affordable?		
Pilot tested the scheme, if at all possible, in a department or division or a representative sample of employees to obtain information on: • how well the formula works? • the appropriateness of the measures? • the cost of the scheme? • its impact? • the effectiveness of the process of making decisions on bonuses (eg the application of performance management)? • the reactions of staff, including confirming that the size of the bonus provides a worthwhile incentive/recognition?		
Made amendments as necessary in the light of the test?		
Defined responsibilities for introducing, maintaining and evaluating the scheme, including processes for ensuring consistency and fairness?		
Prepared a plan for introducing the scheme covering the agreement of performance indicators and targets, methods of reviewing performance, the process of deciding on bonus payments and communications?		
Set a cap on bonus earnings to cover situations where extraordinary but fortuitous results have been achieved?		
Prepared communications materials for employees that describe the purpose of the scheme, how it works and how employees will be affected?		
Ensured that the scheme will be embedded in the organization's day-to-day operating processes, including management reports and performance reviews?		
Ensured that management information is readily available on results so that individuals can track progress against scheme targets?		
Specified whether the scheme is pensionable or non-pensionable (typically the latter)?		
Documented contractual implications, including: • conditions of payment for individuals under notice at year end or payment date? • arrangements for employees on long-term absence? • internal transfers? • voluntary or involuntary terminations? • retirement? • other leavers?		
Specified what scope there is for discretion in interpreting the scheme, by whom and in what circumstances?		
Set a time limit on the operation of the bonus scheme (often one year), on completion of which the scheme may be changed or abandoned?		

Stage 4: Manage scheme

Once in place, a scheme will not manage itself. The essential points to remember when managing the scheme are:

- Ensure that its purpose and methodology are fully understood by staff.
- Keep communicating progress against key performance targets.
- Regularly review performance measures used in the scheme to see that they are business orientated, realistic, and demanding but still attainable.
- Monitor proposals for bonus payments to ensure that they are justified, fair and applied consistently across the organization.
- Measure costs of the scheme against budget and take action to control costs as necessary.

Stage 5: Evaluate scheme

A bonus scheme needs to be reviewed regularly to ensure that it is still achieving the same objectives as when it was introduced. Schemes can degrade over time through lack of communication or change in business circumstances. It cannot be assumed that the scheme will look after itself once it has been introduced. It needs to be evaluated, ideally at the end of each cycle or annually, to:

- measure the costs of the scheme against budget;
- assess the impact of the scheme on performance;
- assess the extent to which the scheme is self-financing;
- review developments in the business and their implications for the scheme;
- in the light of the above, consider any changes required to the scheme's formula or to the key performance indicators used;
- decide whether to end a scheme and whether or not it should be replaced and if so, by what.

A detailed checklist of questions that can be used to audit the effectiveness of a scheme is provided in Figure 9.15.

Another way of checking the effectiveness of bonus arrangements is to ask employees directly, as part of a broader employee survey, as a stand-alone survey or in focus groups. Sample questions are provided in Figure 9.16.

FIGURE 9.15 Checklist: bonus scheme review

Checklist: bonus scheme audit	Yes	No
Does the scheme have a well defined rationale?		
Does it provide a clear line of sight between effort or contribution and the reward?		
Is the scheme related to clear business goals?		
Does the scheme incorporate realistic, significant and measurable key performance indicators (KPIs)?		
Does the scheme provide a clear line of sight between pay and corporate, team or individual performance?		
Is the scheme based on a well established and effective process of performance management for individual bonuses?		
Does the scheme identify the behaviour you want to be encouraged by the scheme?		
Does the scheme set targets that are achievable?		
Are participants being kept up to date with relevant performance measures in order to manage expectations?		
Is the scheme operated fairly, equitably, consistently and transparently?		
Is the scheme appropriate for the type of people to whom it applies?		
Is the scheme reasonably easy to understand and manage, ie not over-complex?		
Is there regular communication about progress against the scheme targets?		
Does the scheme only provide for payment if a demanding threshold of performance is achieved?		
Does the scheme result in meaningful rewards?		
Does the scheme contain arrangements to restrict (cap) the maximum payment to an acceptable sum?		
Is the scheme self-financing?		
Are payments non-pensionable?		
Does the scheme provide scope to moderate the organization-wide element of any bonus by reference to personal performance?		
Is the scheme simple to communicate?		
Does the scheme ensure that mediocre/poor performers are not rewarded?		
Are there clear and published scheme rules?		
Does the scheme provide for review at regular intervals to decide whether it needs to be amended, replaced or cancelled?		
Taking into account the previous questions, does the scheme meet its defined objectives?		

FIGURE 9.16 Employee survey – attitudes to bonus

Employee questionnaire Question	Strongly disagree	Disagree	Neither agree nor disagree	Agree	Strongly agree
I have a clear understanding of how my performance links to my bonus award.					
I have a clear understanding of how my bonus links to the performance of the department/business area.					
I have a clear understanding of how my bonus links to the performance of the organization.					
The bonus scheme has a positive impact on team work and cooperation.					
I am satisfied with the process for determining my bonus.					
The bonus awards are worth striving for.					
I believe the management of the relationship between pay and performance has improved over the last ... years.					
On the whole, the bonus scheme is well designed.					
I understand what my basic salary is for and what my bonus is for.					
Exceptionally good performers should receive more than moderately good performers.					
I am motivated in my job by the prospect of a bonus award.					
The bonus plan makes a difference to the way I go about my work.					
The bonus plan focuses my effort on key performance measures.					
I believe bonus awards are distributed fairly.					
I can expect to receive a bonus award if I perform exceptionally well.					

References

Bonus schemes (2010) Incomes Data Services, London, Study 911, February

Carty, M (2009) IRS bonuses and incentives survey: employers keep the faith in bonuses, *IRS Employment Review*, No 920, April

Egan, J (2009) Bonuses and cash incentives fact sheet May 2009, CIPD, London; available online at www.cipd.co.uk

e-reward 2006 survey of bonus schemes: www.e-reward.co.uk

Schuster, J R and Zingheim, P K (2000) *Pay People Right!: Breakthrough Reward Strategies to Create Great Companies*, Jossey Bass, San Francisco

Tool 10
Executive remuneration

Introduction

Executive remuneration (sometimes called executive compensation) as described in this tool consists of the pay and benefits of executive board directors in private sector companies and of members of the top management team in public or not-for-profit organizations. Executive remuneration policy may be the responsibility of a formally constituted remuneration committee (remcom) which is usually a subcommittee of the main board or governing body. This is generally regarded as good practice and the tool therefore deals with the concerns of such committees. But even where executive reward policy is not handled by a formal remuneration committee, the considerations contained in this tool should still apply.

The principles of executive remuneration

In many ways, the principles affecting executive remuneration are the same as those applying to reward management generally as covered in other tools, for example bonus schemes. The differences are: first, the public visibility of pay decisions and therefore the impact they make on the company's reputation; second, bearing in mind this visibility, the ways in which executive pay policies indicate the quality of corporate governance and the corporate culture; and third, the influence executive pay decisions have on reward policy throughout the organization, for example on the use of variable pay.

The elements of executive remuneration

The elements of executive remuneration are:

- *base pay* – the basic salary of an executive, which may be reviewed annually to reflect perceived market worth or overall contribution;

- *variable pay* – remuneration in addition to base pay in the form of bonuses and longer-term incentives (bonuses) paid in cash or as shares;
- *service contracts* – in the past these could be long term, ie several years, but current practice favours rolling contracts that are more likely to restrict notice periods to up to one year, to avoid excessive severance costs;
- *benefits* – pension schemes and other perquisites such as company cars or healthcare plans.

Purpose of the tool

The purpose of the tool is to provide guidance to chief executives, members of executive boards or management committees, members of remuneration committees, and HR or reward professionals responsible for advising any of the above and for implementing agreed policy and practices. The tool deals with executive reward guiding principles and the major decisions that need to be made on corporate governance (the role and composition of remuneration committees), and on remuneration policies and practices as applied generally or to individual executives.

Contents of the tool

The tool is set out under the following headings:

- Executive remuneration guiding principles;
- The role and use of remuneration committees;
- Total remuneration policy;
- Base pay;
- Bonus schemes;
- Longer-term incentive plans;
- Clawback policy;
- Contracts;
- Pensions and other benefits.

Guiding principles

A decision needs to be made on the principles that should guide a remuneration committee or any other body or individual concerned with executive

FIGURE 10.1 Example: guiding principles, executive remuneration

- The remuneration policy should support the achievement of the organization's business strategy and be clear and simple.
- Executive remuneration policy should foster the organization's values relating to performance, the delivery of high levels of quality and service, promotion of the interests of stakeholders including customers, and social responsibility.
- Levels and methods of remuneration should enable the organization to attract, retain and motivate executives of the quality required to run the company successfully, but the company should avoid paying more than is necessary for this purpose.
- The remuneration committee should judge where to position executive remuneration levels in their company relative to other companies. But they should use such comparisons with caution in view of the risk of an upward ratchet of remuneration levels with no corresponding improvement in performance.
- Incentives should support the achievement of the organization's strategic objectives and the delivery of sustainable value to stakeholders.
- A significant proportion of executives' remuneration should be structured so as to link rewards to corporate and individual performance in order to align their interests with those of stakeholders and to give them keen incentives to perform at the highest levels.
- Bonus payments or share allocations should be subject to challenging performance criteria reflecting the company's objectives. The predominant share (two-thirds or more) of bonuses that exceed a significant level should be paid in a deferred form (deferred cash or shares), with a deferral period that is appropriate to the nature of the business and its risks. Payment of deferred bonuses should be linked to financial performance during the deferral period.
- The financial impact of individual or collective executive remuneration proposals and decisions should be assessed and budgeted for in advance.
- Remuneration policies should be consistent with effective risk management including pension and termination arrangements.
- Arrangements should be made to claw back bonus payments in defined circumstances, eg restatement of financial results.

remuneration on the policies and practices that should be adopted. These principles should be formulated by reference to existing guidelines, for example:

- The Combined Code of Corporate Governance (2008);
- The Turner Review Code of Good Practice (2009);
- The CIPD Principles of Executive Remuneration (2010).

An example of a list of guiding principles is set out in Figure 10.1.

Remuneration committees

The Committee on Corporate Governance (2000) of the Stock Exchange and other reports recommended the establishment of remuneration committees

FIGURE 10.2   Checklist: remuneration committees

Question	Yes	No
• Have members of the remuneration committee (the committee) the appropriate skills, knowledge, understanding of the organization and independence required to come to balanced and dispassionate decisions on remuneration? • Does the committee have written terms of reference? • Are the decisions or recommendations of the committee recorded in writing? • Does the committee act independently? • Is the information made available to the committee by external consultants or HR reliable, relevant, comprehensive and up-to-date?		

to provide an independent basis for setting the salary levels and the rules covering incentives, share options, benefit entitlements and contract provisions for executive directors. It recommended that remuneration committees should:

- be accountable to shareholders;
- be constituted as subcommittees of company boards, and boards should elect both the chairman and the members;
- consist entirely of non-executive directors who have no personal financial interests at stake;
- should set broad policy for executive remuneration as a whole as well as the remuneration packages of executive directors and, sometimes, other senior executives;
- set out in the annual report statements on remuneration policy and the methods used to form that policy, and disclose details of the remuneration of individual directors.

The Combined Code of Corporate Governance (2008) laid down further principles that remuneration committees should take into account when considering pay levels, including the statement that they should avoid paying more than is necessary and be sensitive to pay and employment conditions elsewhere in the organization, especially when determining annual salary increases.

Remuneration committees are now well established as bodies for making recommendations on executive remuneration, often with the advice of remuneration consultants. Points for consideration in setting up and operating a remuneration committee are given in the checklist set out in Figure 10.2. The considerations affecting executive remuneration policy decisions on the basis of recommendations from a remuneration committee (or any other individual or group making proposals) are contained in Figure 10.3.

FIGURE 10.3   Checklist: formulating executive remuneration proposals

Question	Yes	No
• Are the conclusions and recommendations made by the remuneration committee fully supported by the evidence they have assembled?		
• Has sufficient account been taken of the context in which performance takes place in the shape of the short-term objectives and long-term strategy of the organization, its financial situation, its future prospects and its culture?		
• Do recommendations fully take into account the markets in which the organization sources and competes for talent?		
• Has account been taken of the relationship between executive remuneration and that of other employees?		
• Has account been taken of the interests and expectations of all stakeholders?		
• Are realistic costings of proposals available?		
• Has a risk assessment been made of the direct and indirect costs involved under different performance and financial scenarios?		
• Has sufficient attention been paid to the effect of proposals on the image and reputation of the company as reflected in the reactions of the media and major investors?		
• Has sufficient attention been paid to the effect of proposals on the morale and motivation of employees generally (eg the differential between the level of executive pay and that of other staff)?		
• Will the organization be able to produce a convincing rationale to stakeholders for its executive remuneration policies?		

Total remuneration policy

Remuneration committees and those who respond to their recommendations are mainly concerned with setting remuneration levels, but policy decisions are required on the mix in the total remuneration package of base pay, short- and long-term incentives and benefits. A balanced approach to executive remuneration is required in order to obtain the maximum benefit from each of its constituents.

Total remuneration policy should cover:

- A definition of what constitutes total remuneration.
- The objectives of the total remuneration policy. The objectives should be set out as a basis for planning, operation and evaluation. They may refer to attraction and retention, motivation, recognition, the encouragement of desired behaviours, focus on specific goals or setting the pattern of remuneration for other staff.
- The stance of the organization on the relationship between the level of total remuneration and each of its components and the level of market rates. Typical stances include at or above the upper quartile,

at the median or between the median and upper quartile. ▓▓▓ be decided that base pay should have one relationship (say a̲t̲ median) while the variable pay element should be above the median, thus bringing total remuneration to the upper quartile.

- The proportion of base pay to total pay. There is no 'right' proportion, although typically the proportion of variable to the total tends to be much higher for executive directors (eg 50 per cent or more) than for other staff, on the grounds that directors are there to deliver results and are in a key position to do so. It is therefore assumed that they should be incentivized appropriately to achieve those results and rewarded properly when they have been achieved.

- The use of short-term or long-term incentives. If there is an overemphasis on short-term performance rather than long-term performance, inappropriate risk taking or actions that compromise longer-term goal attainment may be encouraged. But if the period is too long, the perceived value of awards can be reduced and cease to be motivational. Policy decisions need to be made on the mix of annual cash bonus schemes that focus on achieving short-term financial and operational goals and longer-term incentive plans consisting of incentive share plans which relate reward to growth in shareholder value, and deferred bonus schemes which only pay out when longer-term success has been achieved. A mix of short- and longer-term incentives may be appropriate to focus both on achieving immediate results and longer-term growth. There is no one-size-fits-all approach, but a range of arrangements should be considered based on the executive's impact on company results, the need to establish a direct link to the creation of shareholder value and the extent to which the executive is expected to take calculated risks.

- The proportion of incentive payments made as cash bonuses or in equities. There is a trend to increase the proportion paid in equities, partly as a result of external pressures to minimize short-termism and excessive risk taking. Providing cash bonus schemes as well as share-based incentives tempers the connection with (and leverage of) share price volatility.

- The differentials between the chief executive and other directors, the differentials, if any, between directors, and the differentials between directors and the next level of management.

Base pay

Base pay is calculated by reference to the market worth of the individual director or senior executive and an assessment of the continuing value of the contribution made by the individual to the company. It is often a spot rate and it can be increased (or, very rarely, decreased) in response to changes in market rates or the perceived value of the executive's contribution. Base pay may be a small proportion of total earnings.

The Association of British Insurers (ABI) in its 2009 guidelines recommends that executive remuneration should be set at levels that retain and motivate, based on selection and interpretation of appropriate benchmarks. However, these should be used with caution, in view of the risk of an upward ratchet of remuneration levels with no corresponding improvement in performance.

In any case organizations should:

- examine carefully assumptions about external base pay comparisons;
- examine the relationship between base pay and pay-at-risk/incentives;
- consider the relationship between executive base pay and pay for other staff, and the impact this has on staff perception of their leadership and on their psychological contract with the organization;
- review carefully pronouncements on pay made by any relevant regulatory or sector bodies.

Bonus schemes

Bonus schemes provide cash incentives and rewards over the short term, typically annually. A checklist of design issues is provided in Figure 10.4 (also see Tool 9 on bonus design).

FIGURE 10.4   Checklist: bonus design

Question	Yes	No
Does the scheme focus on the achievement of key financial and operational goals?		
Is it based on significant, realistic and measurable key performance indicators?		
Does it create a moral hazard, ie an incentive to act inappropriately in pursuit of a high bonus?		
Does it encourage the pursuit of short-term gains or engagement in unduly risky enterprises at the expense of longer-term and sustained success?		
Is there any potential to reward failure?		
Does it pay out only if a demanding threshold of performance is achieved?		
Does it provide for review at regular intervals to decide whether the scheme needs to be amended, replaced or cancelled?		
Is there scope for clawback in defined circumstances?		

Longer-term incentive plans

Defined

Longer-term incentive plans provide for target-related rewards to be paid after a period of two years or more (seldom more than five years). They include share-option schemes, performance share schemes and deferred bonus schemes. Organizations may have more than one scheme.

Aim

Their aim is to motivate executives to achieve the most critical longer-term priorities of the business. Thus they mitigate the short-termism which annual bonus plans may encourage. Longer-term incentive share plans also aim to be responsive to shareholder interests by providing a meaningful relationship between the reward and shareholder value creation.

Choice of equity vehicles

Highly leveraged equity vehicles, such as stock options, provide significant payouts when performance is strong. But this can encourage executives to take excessive risks with hopes of a large payoff, since the downside risk is fixed, regardless of how poor results might be. By granting options in combination with other, less leveraged vehicles (such as performance shares), the equity programme can achieve a more balanced risk–reward profile.

Performance targets and measures

The ABI recommends in its 2009 guidelines that challenging targets should be set that:

- relate to overall corporate performance;
- demonstrate the achievement of a level of financial performance that is demanding and stretching in the context of the prospects for the company and the prevailing economic environment in which it operates;
- can be measured relative to an appropriate defined peer group or other relevant benchmark;
- are disclosed and transparent.

The ABI favours total shareholder return (TSR) relative to a relevant index or peer group as a generally acceptable performance criterion and it is increasingly used for long-term incentive schemes. It means that executives are rewarded for achieving returns to shareholders above the median achieved by other companies. The advantage of TSR is that it establishes a clear linkage with the performance observed by shareholders.

Phasing

The ABI 2009 guidelines note that the regular phasing of share incentive awards and option grants, generally on an annual basis, is strongly encouraged because this:

- reduces the risk of unanticipated outcomes that arise out of share price volatility and cyclical factors;
- eliminates the perceived problem that a limit on subsisting options encourages early exercise;
- allows the adoption of a single performance measurement period;
- lessens the possible incidence of 'underwater' options, where the share price falls below the exercise price.

Criteria for long-term incentives

The criteria for long-term incentives are similar to those listed earlier for bonus schemes. In addition, incentive plans should:

- be linked to individual and corporate performance through graduated targets that align the interests of executives with those of shareholders;
- prohibit automatic entitlement to share-based payments in the event of early termination;
- provide for phased payments;
- be regularly reviewed to ensure their continued effectiveness, compliance with current guidelines and contribution to shareholder value;
- allow inappropriate risk to be managed by providing for caps on payouts;
- not rely unduly, or possibly at all, on highly leveraged share option plans that, because of unforeseeable variations in share value, can result in excessive payouts or demotivate executives when share values are dramatically underwater.

Clawback policy

The ABI 2009 guidelines state: 'Where performance achievements are subsequently found to have been significantly misstated so that bonuses and other incentives should not have been paid, effective avenues of redress should be considered.' In other words, the whole or part of the unearned bonus should be recovered. This can be done through a clawback provision allowing a company to take back previous performance-based payment in defined circumstances. In the United States 72 per cent of Fortune 100 companies had clawback provisions in 2009. The proportion of FTSE companies in the UK with formal clawback policies is probably much smaller. This is because clawback can be highly problematic unless the terms are very carefully defined and are legally watertight. It is necessary to have legal advice in drafting a clawback clause in an employment contract. The events that might trigger a clawback therefore need to be defined with precision at the outset, and be accepted as fair to all. Similarly, the period during which clawback might be invoked must also be clear from the start. Events such as those involving misconduct or serious mismanagement that have a direct impact on the company's financial standing carry the strongest case for triggering a clawback. The basic points to be taken into account in designing a clawback provision are:

- The repayment obligation should be stated clearly in writing and agreed by both parties as part of an employment contract before any bonus or incentive arrangements are made.
- The type of payment to which the clawback relates (eg cash bonus, long-term equity-based incentive) should be defined.
- The individuals to whom the clawback provision applies should be defined, (eg the chief executive, the finance director, all executive directors).
- The events that should trigger a clawback should be defined (eg fraud, misconduct, negligence, poor performance, or culpable conduct that results in incorrect financial information and a material financial restatement).
- How and when clawback should take place on severance.
- The employer should have the discretion to determine the manner and timing of the repayment obligation.
- Who should deal with clawback situations, eg the remuneration committee.

The notion of clawback resonates in a climate where it is believed that excessive and unjustified bonus or incentive payments have been made, but it is not an easy option. There are issues of enforceability and of insufficient funds being available from the executive.

There are alternatives to a clawback provision, such as a retention bonus programme. It can be argued that some organizations have clearly had clawback for some years – in the form of performance-related stock. If an organization doesn't meet its long-term goals, incentives do not vest and therefore major parts of remuneration that were on the table are taken away. Above all, clawback issues can be minimized if the design of the incentive scheme takes account of the risks involved and provides for them by paying out only when targets have been reached successfully. Sound plan design and payment terms are probably the best ways to avoid the need for clawback provisions. Care should also be taken over severance provisions in the executive's contract because it is when executives leave a company that the need for clawback is most likely.

Service contracts

Long-term service contracts for directors have been fairly typical, but they are disliked by institutional investors and regulators because of the high severance payments to departing chief executives and directors that are made if the contract is for two or three years, even when it was suspected or actually the case that they had been voted off the board because of inadequate performance. Rolling contracts for directors are now more likely to be restricted to one year. The ABI 2009 guidelines recommend that the following points should be borne in mind when preparing contracts:

- Remuneration committees should ensure that the policy and objectives on directors' contracts are clearly stated in the remuneration report.
- When drawing up contracts, remuneration committees should calculate the likely cost of any severance and determine whether this is acceptable.
- All payments made should be based upon performance in relation to objectives and take account of the overall financial circumstances of the company.
- Companies should justify their policies on contractual protection.
- Contracts should commit companies not to pay for failure.
- Phased payments are generally appropriate for fulfilling compensation on early termination.
- Shareholders are less supportive of the liquidated damages approach, which involves agreement at the outset on the amount that will be paid in the event of severance.
- Remuneration committees should ensure that full benefit of mitigation is obtained. This includes the legal obligation on the part of the outgoing director to mitigate the loss incurred through severance by seeking other employment and reducing the need for compensation.
- Contracts should make clear that if a director is dismissed as a result of a disciplinary procedure, a shorter notice period than that given in the contract would apply.
- Contracts should not provide additional protection in the form of compensation for severance as a result of change of control.
- Pension entitlement on severance can represent a large element of cost to shareholders. Remuneration committees should identify, review and disclose in their report any arrangements that guarantee

pensions with limited or no abatement on severance or early retirement. These would not be regarded as acceptable if included in new contracts.

- Remuneration committees should demonstrate that the route taken on severance represents the lowest overall cost to the company.

Pensions and other benefits

Employee benefits for executives may amount to over 20 per cent of the total reward package. The most important element is the pension scheme, and where final salary schemes are still in place directors may be provided with a much higher accrual rate than is typical. This means that the maximum two-thirds pension may be achieved after 20 years' service or even less, rather than the 40 years it takes in a typical one-sixtieth scheme. Pensions can also be inflated, by presenting the departing director with a last-minute substantial increase in pensionable salary. The following points should be considered when making pension and other benefit provisions:

- The organization should understand the current and future cost of its pension and benefits provisions and how the pension will be funded. In particular, the long-term costs of any contractual commitments that enhance an executive's pension entitlement should be calculated.
- The risk to the reputation of the organization in unduly enhancing the pensions of departing executives as well as the costs incurred should be considered.
- Pensions and other benefits, including post-retirement benefits, should be reviewed regularly to ensure that they are justified.
- A time limit should be applied to all benefits.

References

Combined Code on Corporate Governance (2008) The Financial Reporting Council, London

Combined Code: Principles of good governance and code of best practice (2000) Committee on Corporate Governance, Stock Exchange, London

Guidelines on Executive Remuneration (2009) Association of British Insurers, London

Greenbury, R (1995) *Report of the Study Group on Directors' Remuneration*, Gee Publishing, London

Principles of Executive Remuneration (2010) Chartered Institute of Personnel and Development, London; www.CIPD.co.uk/principles of executive remuneration

Turner, A (2009) *The Turner Review; A regulatory response to the banking crisis*, Financial Services Authority, London

Tool 11
International reward

Introduction

International reward management is the process of rewarding people in international or multinational organizations. It involves the worldwide management of rewards as well as managing the remuneration of expatriates.

In developing reward strategies for international firms it is necessary to decide on the extent to which a firm wants to achieve consistency of practice in accordance with group policy (convergence) or to allow an appropriate degree of freedom in local firms to develop reward policies and practices that fit their country's characteristics and culture and are in line with local circumstances and culture (divergence). There is a tension between the desire to pursue a global good-practice policy and the pressure for local best fit. A compromise may be reached between extreme convergence or divergence by encouraging flexibility within a framework – allowing some freedom to local companies as long as they conform to group reward guiding principles.

Purpose of the tool

The purpose of the tool is to provide a basis for reward and HR practitioners to review and develop reward strategies and practices on an international basis. It covers:

- The development of international reward guiding principles;
- The conduct of surveys into international reward practice in a global organization;

- Conducting a gap analysis on the differences between reward policy and practice in the parent company and the policies and practices of local companies or units;
- Policy on convergence or divergence;
- Guidelines on rewarding expatriates.

International reward strategy guiding principles

International reward strategy is concerned with the development of an integrated approach to building reward policies and practices across international boundaries. It should be integrated in the sense that it takes into account the business goals and drivers of the parent company while at the same time fitting the strategy to the different contexts and cultures across the globe. The issue of the extent to which the reward strategy should be centralized or decentralized (convergence or divergence) needs to be addressed. The strategy should be based on guiding principles and should cover all aspects of reward management.

FIGURE 11.1   International reward guiding principles

Possible guideline content	Agreed guideline content
The balance between convergence and divergence in the application of reward policies	
The importance attached to a total rewards approach	
The use of job evaluation to provide for internal equity	
The relationship between levels of pay in the local company and local market rates	
The degree of flexibility present in base pay management (grade and pay structures)	
The need for a common performance management system	
The scope for pay progression	
The importance attached to paying for performance	
The use of variable pay – short-, medium- and long-term incentives	
The use of forms of recognition other than pay	
The use of flexible benefits	
The basis upon which expatriates and third-country nationals should be paid	

Guiding principles for international reward can be considered under the policy headings set out in Figure 11.1. This could be used as an agenda for discussion with interested parties.

Survey of reward programmes

The features of the reward programmes in the parent company and each international location need to be surveyed as the basis for conducting a gap analysis to identify any differences and decide in the light of the guiding principles what actions need to be taken in developing a global reward strategy. For each country the survey should cover basic details of the employee populations and their rates of pay compared with local rates (Figure 11.2) and information on the main aspects of reward policy and practice (Figure 11.3).

Gap analysis

The gap analysis shown in Figure 11.4 compares the differences between policy and practice in the parent company and those in overseas subsidiaries or locations. This provides a basis for deciding what changes, if any, are required in the overseas location to bring them into line with practices in headquarters. This decision will be affected by general considerations relating to convergence and divergence as covered below.

Convergence/divergence policy

Total convergence means that reward policies and practices are basically the same in all locations (except on the rates of pay as affected by the local market). Total divergence means that reward policies and practices are differentiated in response to local requirements. There can be degrees of convergence or divergence. The factors affecting choice (convergence/divergence) are:

- the extent to which there are well-defined local norms;
- the degree to which an operating unit is embedded in the local environment;
- the strength of the flow of resources – finance, information and people – between the parent and the subsidiary;
- the orientation of the parent to control;
- the nature of the industry – the extent to which it is primarily a domestic industry at local level;
- the specific organizational competences, including HR management, that are critical for achieving competitive advantage in a global environment.

FIGURE 11.2   Survey of employee numbers and rates of pay

Name and location of company/unit		Average pay (£)	Median market rate (£)
Employee category	Number*	Average pay (£)	Median market rate (£)
Directors or members of senior management team	Local staff		
	Expatriates or third-country nationals		–
Senior managers in charge of a major function	Local staff		
	Expatriates or third-country nationals		–
Middle managers in charge of a small function or reporting to a senior manager	Local staff		
	Expatriates or third-country nationals		–
Junior managers or team leaders in charge of a team of employees	Local staff		
	Expatriates or third-country nationals		–
Senior professional and technical staff	Local staff		
	Expatriates or third-country nationals		–
Professional and technical staff	Local staff		
	Expatriates or third-country nationals		–
Senior administrative staff	Local staff		
	Expatriates or third-country nationals		–
Administrative staff/ administrative assistants	Local staff		
	Expatriates or third-country nationals		–
Senior sales and customer service staff	Local staff		
	Expatriates or third-country nationals		–
Sales and customer service staff	Local staff		
	Expatriates or third-country nationals		–
Senior service staff, eg security, maintenance, cleaning, catering	Local staff		
	Expatriates or third-country nationals		–
Service staff, eg security, maintenance, cleaning, catering	Local staff		
	Expatriates or third-country nationals		–
Skilled manual workers	Local staff		
	Expatriates or third-country nationals		–
Semi-skilled manual workers	Local staff		
	Expatriates or third-country nationals		–
Unskilled manual workers	Local staff		
	Expatriates or third-country nationals		–

*full-time and full-time equivalent

FIGURE 11.3 Analysis of reward policies and practices

Reward area	Policy/practice	Tick yes or no		Information required if yes
		Yes	No	
Overall reward strategy/ policy	Written reward strategy			Details of strategy
	Total rewards approach			Details of approach
	Market stance policy			Policy on market position, eg median
Performance management	Formal system			Details of performance management system
Job evaluation	Formal job evaluation scheme			Details of type of scheme
Base pay management	Formal grade and pay structure			Type of structure, including number of bands or grades
Contingent pay	Formal scheme for rewarding employees according to performance, contribution or skill			Type of scheme
Variable pay	Bonuses and long-term incentives			Types of schemes
Recognition	Formal recognition scheme			Details of scheme
Employee benefits	Sick pay			Details of provision
	Permanent health insurance			
	Childcare			
	Company car			
	Financial assistance			
	Others			
	Flexible benefits			Details of scheme
Pensions	Company-provided occupational pensions scheme			Details of scheme
Expatriate rewards	Home pay			Further information on how policy applied including dealing with third-country nationals
	Host pay			

Supporting information

Indicate any contextual factors that affect reward policy and practice, eg labour and employment legislation, the country's labour market, industrial relations (impact of trade unions), custom and practice in the country, cultural influences.

FIGURE 11.4 Gap analysis of reward policies and practices

		Policy/practice in parent company (yes/no)	Policy/practice in overseas locations (yes/no)				
			A	B	C	D	E
Overall reward strategy/ policy	Written reward strategy						
	Total rewards approach						
	Market stance policy						
Performance management	Formal system						
Job evaluation	Formal job evaluation scheme						
Base pay management	Formal grade and pay structure						
Contingent pay	Formal scheme for rewarding employees according to performance, contribution or skill						
Variable pay	Bonuses and long-term incentives						
Recognition	Formal recognition scheme						
Employee benefits	Sick pay						
	Permanent health insurance						
	Child care						
	Company car						
	Financial assistance						
	Others						
	Flexible benefits						
Pensions	Company-provided occupational pensions scheme						
Expatriate rewards	Home pay						
	Host pay						

Arguments for and against convergence (centralization)

FIGURE 11.5   Arguments for and against convergence (centralization)

Arguments for	Arguments against
• Improved management and control of rewards • Consistent link between rewards and results/behaviour • Consistent position versus the market • Internal equity • Develop common culture • Talent mobility • Ability to leverage purchasing power for benefits	• Ignores local contextual considerations (culture, legislation, etc) • Inhibits local initiatives • Problem of developing and maintaining an entirely consistent set of reward policies and practices, bearing in mind differences • Potential cost

Arguments for and against divergence (decentralization)

FIGURE 11.6   Arguments for and against divergence (decentralization)

Arguments for	Arguments against
• Respect local contextual considerations • Recognition that the policies and practices at headquarters may be suitable for the environment there but will not travel easily elsewhere • Enable local management to respond to and accommodate local requirements • Provide scope to local management to exercise initiative • Recognize the quality of local management and their ability to make sensible decisions	• Practices proved to be effective at headquarters not exported to the advantage of local units • Inconsistencies in the application of reward policies and practices • Increase problems of moving expatriates and third-country nationals to and between different locations • Increased problems of managing reward worldwide

Even if the arguments for convergence carry the day, it is obviously necessary for overseas companies to comply with local employment law and to set reward levels in relation to local market rates. Convergence may therefore focus solely on core reward policies or practices such as job evaluation, performance management, base pay management, contingent pay or long-term incentives. Five levels of convergence can be identified as set out in Figure 11.7.

FIGURE 11.7   Levels of convergence and divergence in
international reward policies and practices

Level 1: total convergence	Central reward policies and practices have to be followed by each operating unit. These may include a standard job evaluation scheme, uniform grade and pay structure (with scope for local market differentiation), common approach to incentives and a common set of benefits.
Level 2: partial convergence	Central reward policies are applied in some but not all aspects of reward management. Centralization may be limited to senior management or international staff (expatriates or nationals from countries other than the parent company working in the local country – third-country nationals). Reward policies and practices for local nationals are decentralized.
Level 3: partial divergence	Corporate job evaluation schemes and grade structures are recommended but modification is permitted to fit local conditions. However, all locations are expected to comply with the international guiding principles for reward. There may still be centralized policies for senior managers, expatriates and third-country nationals, and some benefits may be standardized. But pay levels, pay progression and incentive arrangements are determined locally.
Level 4: divergence in line with guiding principles	Complete divergence is allowed with regard to reward practices but the local company or unit is required to comply with corporate guiding principles, ie they are allowed flexibility within a framework.
Level 5: total divergence	Local companies have complete freedom to develop and apply their own reward policies and practices, although they will be made aware of the international guiding principles.

Remuneration of expatriates

Policy

Expatriate remuneration arrangements should be based on a set of policy propositions such as the following:

- Expatriates should not be worse off as a result of working abroad; neither should they be significantly better off for doing essentially the same job, although they may be compensated for the extra demands made overseas or for the living and working conditions there.
- Home-country living standards should be maintained as far as possible.
- Higher responsibility should be reflected in the salary paid (this may be a notional home salary).
- The remuneration package should be competitive.

- In developing the remuneration package, particular care has to be taken to giving proper consideration to the conditions under which the employee will be working abroad.

- Account should be taken of the need to maintain equity as far as possible in remuneration between expatriates, some of whom may be from different countries.

- Account also has to be taken of the impact of expatriate pay policies on nationals in the country in which they are working, particularly the problems that can arise when expatriates are paid more than local country nationals who are in similar jobs.

- The package should be cost effective, ie the contribution made by expatriates should justify the total cost of maintaining them abroad – assignment costs can total three or four times the equivalent package in the home country.

Pay

There are four approaches to calculating expatriate pay: home country, host country, selected country and hybrid.

Home-country basis

The home-based method (sometimes called the balance sheet approach) 'builds up' the salary to be paid to the expatriate in the following steps:

1 Determine the salary that would be paid for the expatriate's job in the home country net of income tax and national insurance contributions.

2 Calculate the 'home-country spendable' or net disposable income. This is the portion of income used for day-to-day expenditure at home.

3 Apply a cost of living index to the 'host country expendable income' to give the equivalent buying power in the host country. This is used as a measure of expenditure levels in the host country and is an important yardstick that is used to ensure that the expatriate will be no worse off abroad than at home. There are various providers of COLA (cost of living adjustment) indices, such as ORC Worldwide and PricewaterhouseCoopers.

4 Add extra allowances for working abroad (see below).

This is the most popular approach.

Host-country basis

This involves paying the market rate for the job in the host country. Allowances may be paid for the expenditure incurred by expatriates because they are living abroad, eg second-home costs, children's education.

Selected country basis

The salary structure in a selected country (often where the company's head-quarters are sited) provides the base and this is built up as in the home-country method.

Hybrid basis

This approach divides the expatriate's salary into two components. One – the local component – is the same for all expatriates working in jobs at the same level irrespective of their country of origin. The other local component is based on a calculation of the spendable income in the host country required to maintain a home-country standard of living.

Choice of approach

The choice is often between the two most popular approaches – the home- and host-based methods. Their advantages and disadvantages are set out in Figure 11.8.

FIGURE 11.8   Advantages and disadvantages of the home- and host-based methods of paying expatriates

Method	*Advantages*	*Disadvantages*
Home based	• Ensures that expatriates do not lose out by working abroad • Easy to communicate to expatriates • Easier to slot back into home-country salary on return • Particularly appropriate for shorter assignments after which the employee will return home	• Expatriates may be paid significantly more than local nationals doing the same jobs, thereby causing dissatisfaction and possible friction • More difficult to apply when transfers are to less-developed countries • In effect there will be two reward systems in the same country, which can cause confusion • May need transition plan to localize arrangements for long-serving expatriates
Host based	• Avoids the possible dissatisfaction and friction that can arise when expatriates are paid significantly more than local nationals doing the same jobs • Enables one coherent pay system to be maintained • Easier to apply when transfers are across developed countries	• Expatriates might lose out, making it more difficult to persuade people to work abroad • May be harder to assimilate expatriates back into their own country's pay systems

The choice will depend upon the organization's convergence or divergence strategy. To a large extent it also depends on how important it is to encourage people to work overseas for limited duration assignments and how much importance is attached to ensuring the motivation and commitment of the host-country staff.

Allowances

Although in recent years companies have sought to trim expensive expatriate packages, companies may add a number of allowances as described below to the expatriate's salary to calculate the total expatriate remuneration package. They are designed to compensate for disruption and to make the assignment attractive to the employee. Most are applied to the notional home salary but one of them, the cost of living allowance, is based on spendable income.

The allowances are:

- Cost of living allowance. This is calculated by applying an index to the home-country spendable income. The index measures the relative cost, in the host country, of purchasing conventional 'shopping basket' items, such as food and clothing.

- Exchange rate protection: an allowance or adjustment to pay in the event of volatile currency movements.

- Incentive premium. This offers the expatriate a financial inducement to accept the assignment. It may be intended to compensate for disruption to family life. But companies are tending to reduce this premium or do away with it altogether, particularly for intra-European assignments. They are questioning why an employee should receive 10 to 15 per cent of gross salary for simply moving from one country to another culturally similar one when no such allowance would be payable in the case of a relocation within the UK.

- Hardship allowance. This compensates for discomfort and difficulty in the host country, such as an unpleasant climate, health hazards, poor communications, isolation, language difficulties, risk and poor amenities.

- Separation allowance. This may be paid if expatriates cannot take their family abroad.

- Clothing allowance. A payment for special clothing and accessories that expatriates may need to buy.

- Relocation allowance. This covers the cost of expenses arising when moving from one country to another.

- Housing/utilities. Any additional costs of accommodation or utilities.

Benefits

In addition to support provided in making the transfer (such as immigration/
visa assistance, disturbance/relocation allowance,) the benefits provided to
expatriates may include a range of the following:

- cars (whether for reasons of personal security or to maintain
  home-country entitlement);
- school fees;
- home leave;
- rest and recuperation leave if the expatriate is working in a
  high-hardship territory;
- medical insurance;
- family assistance (to support assimilation in new country);
- taxation equalization or protection (the aim of equalization is that
  assignees continue to pay the same amount of tax as they would have
  done had they remained in the home country, with the employer
  charging a 'hypothetical' tax to the employee and bearing all the
  costs directly; tax protection aims to reimburse employees if their
  total tax liability is higher than it would have been in the home
  country alone);
- language training.

Evaluation

Where existing international remuneration arrangements are in place, they
need to be monitored to ensure that they support the transfer of skills across
the organization, while being cost effective. The following questions form
the basis for a review:

- Are our arrangements adequate to ensure that we have an adequate
  supply of appropriate transferees?
- Based on the countries between which staff transfer, do we have an
  appropriate range of arrangements (eg host country for selected
  markets only) to ensure that we have the most cost-effective
  approach to suit a range of situations (eg strategic, career
  development, self-requested and short-term moves), or is there a case
  for more standardization?
- Do our arrangements continue to reflect the organization's business
  needs, culture and ethos?
- Have we considered other options to long-term assignments,
  eg cheaper short-term assignments?

Tool 12
Employee benefits

Introduction

Employee benefits consist of arrangements made by employers for their employees that enhance the latters' well-being. They are provided in addition to pay and form important elements of the total reward package. As part of total remuneration, they may be deferred or contingent, like a pension scheme, insurance cover or sick pay, or they may be immediate, like a company car or a loan. Employee benefits also include holidays and leave arrangements that are part of an employee's terms and conditions of employment but not strictly remuneration. Some benefits are referred to as 'perks' (perquisites) or 'fringe benefits', but usually only those benefits that extend beyond the core pensions and health benefits, most typically to senior executives.

Employee benefits are a costly part of the remuneration package. They can amount to one-third or more of basic pay costs and therefore have to be planned and managed with care. But they are not all equally wanted or appreciated by the staff that receive them and, from the employer's point of view, some benefits will therefore not provide value for money. This issue can be addressed by the introduction of flexible benefits as described in this tool.

Note that many benefits such as company cars, interest-free loans, private medical insurance, and prizes, gifts and vouchers are taxable. It is worth seeking advice from a tax specialist if in any doubt.

Purpose and contents of the tool

The considerable expense, not to speak of the time and trouble, that can be involved in providing employee benefits, and the fact that they are often under-appreciated and underused, makes it imperative to be clear about what the organization is trying to achieve, ie its employee benefit objectives, and to review the effectiveness of its employee benefits policies and practices against those objectives.

The purpose of this tool is to provide guidance on methods of doing this. The tool is set out in the following sections:

- Conducting a benefits review;
- Defining objectives;
- Reviewing benefit arrangements;
- Developing the benefits package;
- Introducing flexible benefits;
- Communicating to employees.

Conducting an employee benefits review

The steps required to carry out a review of employee benefits are illustrated in Figure 12.1. Note that involving employees plays an important part. As they are the beneficiaries, it is vital to get their views on what they want

FIGURE 12.1   Review of employee benefits

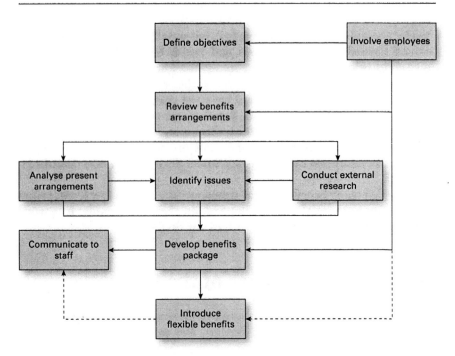

and what they feel about present arrangements, particularly as the perceived value of some benefits is out of proportion with the cost of providing these benefits.

Defining employee benefit objectives

The objectives of employee benefits need to be defined as a basis for formulating benefits policies, developing the benefits package and evaluating the impact of employee benefits. The questionnaire set out in Figure 12.2 includes a number of possible headings and can be used for this purpose.

FIGURE 12.2 Questionnaire: objectives of benefits

Possible objective	Agreed (tick) or disagreed (cross)	Possible rewording if agreed
Contribute to the provision of a competitive total reward package and a compelling employee value proposition and therefore help to attract and retain employees		
Provide for the needs of employees		
Increase employee engagement		
Provide a tax efficient method of remuneration		
Support the achievement of business objectives		
Provide benefits more cheaply than employees can		
Meet the moral responsibility of the organization to provide the benefit		
Enhance the reputation of the organization as a good employer		
Ensure that the policies and practices used to achieve objectives are cost effective		
Meet competitive practice		
Others		

Reviewing employee benefits arrangements

The review of employee benefit arrangements should be divided into the following parts:

- an analysis of current arrangements;
- a review of practices elsewhere (external research);
- on the basis of the above analysis and review, an identification of the issues to be addressed in improving the effectiveness of the organization's policies and practices.

Analysis of current arrangements

The analysis of current arrangements should include:

- the collection of data on the range of benefits offered, their take-up by employees and their cost; the latter may often have to be estimated; professional advisors can help (Figure 12.3);
- an assessment of the effectiveness of benefits policies and practices against agreed objectives; this should be done in conjunction with employees through surveys, focus groups and workshops (Figure 12.4);
- a survey of the views of employees about the benefits package (Figures 12.5 and 12.6);
- an analysis of the preferences of employees (Figures 12.7, 12.8 and 12.9).

Range of benefits offered

FIGURE 12.3 Analysis of employee benefit arrangements

Benefit group	Type of benefit	Available – to all employees or to specified categories of staff	Take-up (percentage of eligible employees)	Annual cost (£)
Occupational pension scheme	Defined benefit (final or average salary scheme)			
	Defined contribution			
	Group personal pension			
	Stakeholder pension			
	Additional voluntary contributions			
Personal security	Life insurance			
	Group income protection (permanent health insurance)			
	Private medical insurance			
	Private dental insurance			
	Health screening			
	Sick pay			
Personal needs (employee well-being)	Childcare			
	Employee assistance programme (EAP)			
	Holidays (above statutory minimum)			
	Membership fees for professional bodies			
	Subsidized meals			
	Bicycle loans (bikes to work)			
	Sport and social facilities			
	Gym subscription			
	Voluntary benefits			
	Concierge scheme			
Financial assistance	Company loans			
	Season ticket loans			
	Mortgage assistance			
	Relocation costs			
Perks	Company car			
	Subsidized petrol			
	Car parking			
	Mobile phones			
Costs	Total cost of benefits			
	Total payroll cost (excluding benefits)			
	Percentage of benefits costs to total payroll costs			

Assessment of the effectiveness of benefits policy and practice

FIGURE 12.4 Questionnaire – extent to which benefit provisions meet objectives

Type of benefit	Objective: score 1–5 where 1 = unachieved, 5 = fully achieved									Total score
	Competitive total reward package	Meet employee needs	Increase engagement	Tax efficient	Help achieve business goals	Provide cheaper benefits for staff	Meet moral responsibility of employer	Enhance employer's reputation	Cost effective	
Pension scheme										
Life insurance										
Group income protection (permanent health insurance)										
Private medical insurance										
Private dental insurance										
Health screening										
Sick pay										
Childcare										
EAP										
Holidays										
Membership fees										
Subsidized meals										
Bicycle loans										
Sport and social facilities										
Gym subscription										
Voluntary benefits										
Concierge scheme										
Company loans										
Season ticket loans										
Mortgage assistance										
Relocation costs										
Company car										
Subsidized petrol										
Car parking										
Mobile phones										

FIGURE 12.5   Questionnaire: employee opinions on the benefits package

	Fully agree	Partially agree	Neither agree nor disagree	Partially disagree	Fully disagree
I am entirely satisfied with the benefits provided by the organization.					
I think the benefits package compares very favourably with what I could get elsewhere.					
I think the level of benefits provided by the organization is too low.					
I am quite clear about the benefits provided by the organization.					
I am satisfied with the range of benefits provided by the organization.					
I appreciate that the organization is going to considerable expense to provide benefits to employees.					
I think I should have some choice over the benefits I receive.					
Too many of the benefits offered by the organization are irrelevant to my needs.					
My organization does a good job of communicating the benefits package.					

Employee opinions

A questionnaire seeking employee opinions about the benefits package is set out in Figure 12.5.

Employee preferences

Employees can be asked in focus groups or workshops or through online surveys to express preferences on the types of benefits they want. An employee questionnaire is given in Figure 12.6.

FIGURE 12.6 Questionnaire: employee benefits preferences

How important are the following aspects of your employment to you and to what extent are they meeting your expectations? Please answer both parts of the question using the following scale: *1 = to a very great extent* *2 = to a great extent* *3 = to some extent/neutral* *4 = to a little extent* *5 = to a very little extent*											
Aspect of employment	*Importance to you*						*Your expectations are being met*				
	1	2	3	4	5		1	2	3	4	5
A competitive base salary											
Pension											
Company car: *score only if currently applicable*											
Health benefits											
Death in service cover											
Permanent health insurance (prolonged disability cover)											
Flexibility of working hours											
Holidays											
Childcare support											
Support to deal with care for other family members											
Staff discounts											
Volunteering opportunities											
Access to fitness facilities											
Learning and development opportunities											
Encouraging a healthy lifestyle											
Personal recognition (non-monetary)											
Other (please specify)											

External research

External research establishes what other organizations are doing about employee benefits, to indicate what is regarded as good practice and to establish the organization's competitive position. The research could involve conducting special surveys of comparable organizations, studying published salary surveys and examining the outcome of surveys by, for example, *Employee Benefits* magazine (**www.employeebenefits.co.uk**).

Developing employee benefits package

Developing the package involves taking account of the outcomes of the review and the key issues that have emerged. Employees should take part in the development programme through workshops and membership of project teams.

Dealing with key issues

Examples of the key issues that might be identified in a benefits review together with possible ways of dealing with them and the factors to be taken into account are given in Figure 12.7.

Contents of the package

Dealing with the issues provides the basis for developing the employee benefits package. This usually consists of a number of core benefits, eg pension scheme, sick pay, life insurance, permanent health insurance and childcare vouchers. To these may be added a voluntary benefits scheme. The opportunity may be given to take a salary sacrifice option that may apply to certain pension rights and, typically, childcare vouchers. A flexible benefits scheme may be incorporated.

As the list of benefits given in Figure 12.3 indicates, there is a huge choice of additional benefits. The availability of too many benefits in a package creates administrative and cost problems and diminishing returns in the shape of appreciation from employees. How many benefits there are will depend on how the benefits package is structured (eg fixed package versus flexibility) and the cost of provision.

Introducing flexible benefits

A flexible benefits scheme (often referred to as 'flex') is an arrangement that allows employees to decide, within certain limits, on the make-up of their benefits package. For employers it is a means of:

- ensuring that rewards match the needs of an increasingly diverse, demanding and ageing workforce;
- getting value for money through better targeting of benefits to employees;

FIGURE 12.7   Dealing with employee benefits issues

Issue	Possible approaches to dealing with issue	Factors to be taken into account	Suggested approach
Benefits package too costly	Reduce range of benefits Reduce scale of benefits Reduce size of employer contribution Introduce flexible benefits Introduce salary sacrifice for selected tax efficient benefits Renegotiate terms with providers Seek alternative less expensive providers Switch from defined benefit pension scheme to defined contribution Self-insure some benefits (only likely to be feasible for large employers)	Impact on employee engagement and morale Impact on reputation of organization Impact on competitive position Impact on ability to attract and retain staff	
Increase perceived value of benefits package	Communicate value to employees (total reward statements, etc) Survey employee opinions and amend aspects of the package to meet their needs Introduce flexible benefits	Getting a convincing message across Problem of identifying what benefits will be valued most Potential increase in costs and complexity of administration	
Employees do not understand the benefits package	Communicate information through various media, especially total reward statements Involve employees in workshops to explore benefits issues Introduce self-service for employees so they can obtain information about their own benefits	Complex packages increase the difficulty of communications Quite a lot of effort is required to communicate	
Benefits package uncompetitive	Benchmark policy of comparable organizations Survey employee opinions on what does or does not attract them about the existing benefits package Upgrade benefits that are demonstrably uncompetitive	Problem of cost-effectiveness – the costs may increase but will the effectiveness of the package as a means of attracting and retaining staff justify the expense? Problem of selecting which benefits to upgrade or introduce – how will their potential effectiveness be assessed?	
Administrative costs too high	Simplify package Switch to external provider for certain aspects of package Change to less expensive external provider	Simplification of package may reduce its impact External provider must be selected carefully to ensure that good service will be provided – review offers from different providers Be clear about internal administrative costs and compare with those of external provider before making a commitment (external provision may be more expensive for small organizations)	

- making the employee benefits package more visible;
- enhancing the perceived value of the benefits package;
- harmonizing and rationalizing benefits;
- enabling them to offer staff additional choice from existing benefits funding where employees are allowed to trade down some benefits cover in return for cash.

For employees, flex can:

- tailor their benefits to personal circumstances;
- improve choice;
- provide an opportunity to trade down some benefits cover to meet their needs for cash.

How flexible benefit schemes work

The main features of a typical cash-based flexible benefit scheme are:

- employees are given a choice within limits of the type or scale of benefits offered to them by their employers;
- employees can vary the size of a chosen benefit;
- each employee is provided with the cash value of their existing benefits, together with a menu of benefits and cash in a preference form (electronic or paper);
- employees are advised of the current level of their benefits and the 'cost' of buying or selling these to suit their individual needs;
- there is typically a limit set on how much of the salary can be used to buy extra benefits;
- employees choose the combination of cash and benefits that suits them;
- it is usual to require employees to retain certain core benefits such as a minimum amount of holiday, accident insurance and life cover;
- a benefits statement is issued to employees as a record of what they have chosen;
- employees can alter their choices at fixed regular intervals (usually once a year), subject to any long-term commitments such as cars and some insured benefits; they can also alter the size of a chosen benefit;
- employees agree as a condition of participating in the flex plan that the menu of benefits, the prices of the benefits and the benefits allowance can all change from year to year;
- some benefits, for example childcare vouchers or health insurance, will be made available from outside providers who in certain cases may charge a licensing fee.

An alternative arrangement is to use a points plan, where each benefit has a points rating and the employee has an allowance of a certain number of points.

Cost of flexible benefits

The advantages of flexible benefits are obvious but the costs involved are considerable, including communicating the concept to staff and continuing administrative costs if an external provider is used. Licence fees based on the number of employees covered may be incurred. At this stage, preliminary enquiries can be made with external advisors on the likely costs that will be incurred. The cost analysis can be summarized on the form illustrated in Figure 12.8.

FIGURE 12.8   Flexible benefits cost analysis

Cost heading	Start-up costs (£)	Ongoing annual costs (£)
Benefits provision		
Professional advice		
Software		
Licensing fees		
Internal administration		
Employee consultation		
Employee communications		
Minus annual national insurance savings (if salary sacrifice introduced)	–	
Total costs		

Assessment of returns from flexible benefits

If salary sacrifice is introduced as part of flexible benefits, there are quantifiable savings to be made. A growing number of employers are introducing salary sacrifice in order to save money on national insurance contributions, and for their employees to save on tax and national insurance. In addition, flexible benefits can save costs arising from recruitment, labour turnover, absenteeism and training. These can be calculated, although it may be difficult to attribute any savings directly to flex, and a qualitative assessment may have to be made. Flex can increase engagement (improvements in that can be measured), support talent management and generally enhance the employee value proposition and the employer brand.

Developing flexible benefits

Flexible benefit schemes should not be over-complex, otherwise employees will be unable to understand them and the take-up will be too low to justify the scheme's existence. But there are many considerations to be taken into account in designing the scheme and planning how to administer it. To develop a fully fledged scheme, ie one offering a range of benefit choices to employees, it is generally essential or at least highly desirable to obtain professional help. It is often best to involve external providers who can offer:

- advice on what is good practice;
- legal and taxation advice;
- the software required;
- a separate administrative centre that relieves the burden from HR;
- help in monitoring and evaluating the package.

The points to be covered in developing a scheme are reviewed below.

The overall design of the scheme

The overall design involves deciding on the core benefits that have to be maintained, identifying benefits that can be flexed, deciding on any limits to the extent to which these benefits can be flexed, costing the benefits as necessary to enable menus to be produced and flex funds set up, if appropriate, and considering how the scheme should be administered.

Cash or points?

Most schemes show each of the benefits with a cash value and the employee uses this as the basis for calculating the effect of their choices. Other schemes use a points plan, where each benefit has a points rating and the employee has an allowance of a certain number of points.

The advantage of showing a cash value is that it gives employees an idea of what the benefit is truly worth and the cost that the employer is bearing. The danger of a cash system is that it may encourage employees to feel that they are being forced to buy benefits out of their own salary.

Whether or not a points or a cash value scheme is used, schemes make a clear distinction between notional or reference salary and the final value of salary that is actually paid in the year, including benefit allowances (regardless of whether this is higher or lower than the notional salary). The notional salary continues to be used as the basis for items such as pension calculations and salary reviews.

Choice of benefits

When deciding on the benefits to be covered by the scheme, some core benefits may be excluded, such as a minimum level of pension provision and life insurance.

Apart from these, there is plenty of choice on which benefits to include. Employee opinion is one of the most important factors to be considered. The starting point will be the existing range of benefits but it may be appropriate to amend this list when introducing flex, bearing in mind the views of employees. Typically, no less than three benefits are included in the flex plan. Offering more than 10 benefits increases the complexity of administration and making choices. When initiating a scheme it may be best to keep it simple by restricting the number of benefits that can be flexed. Others can be added later as the scheme settles in. The CIPD 2009 survey established that the following were the most frequently included benefits in order of popularity:

- dental insurance;
- childcare vouchers;
- critical illness insurance;
- cycle to work scheme;
- health screening;
- private medical insurance;
- healthcare cash plans;
- permanent health insurance;
- life assurance;
- gym subscriptions.

A 2008 IDS benefits review produced broadly the same results, but included holiday flexibility as one of the top benefits provided.

Method of making choices

Once the scheme has been agreed, the choice of benefits is presented to the employees. To ensure a positive reception, it is important that the choices (and the implications of those choices) are clear. If the options are too complicated, or the method of making the choices is perceived as being difficult, then employees will simply default to their existing benefits package and much of the time and money spent in introducing the scheme will have been wasted.

Communicating to employees

Employees and their representatives should be informed about the objectives and policies that drive the employee benefits system. They should understand the grade and pay structure, how grading decisions are made, including the job evaluation system, how their pay can progress within the structure, the basis upon which contingent pay increases are determined and policies on the provision of benefits.

Employees need to be convinced that the system is fair and how employee benefit policies will affect them directly. Individual employees should be informed of the value of the benefits they receive so that they are aware of their total remuneration and, if appropriate, how they can exercise choice over the range or scale of their benefits through a flexible benefits scheme.

Total reward statements communicate to employees the value of the employee benefits such as pensions, holidays, company cars, free car parking and subsidized meals they receive in addition to their pay. They can also be used to describe any other rewards they get such as learning and development opportunities. The aim is to ensure that employees appreciate the total value of their reward package. Too often, people are unaware of what they obtain in addition to their pay. Figure 12.9 shows a simple example of how a total reward statement can be set out. Professional advice may be needed to agree costs and assumptions, for example about whether amounts shown are based on the employee providing this benefit for themselves or actual cost to employer.

In addition to total rewards statements, as many means as possible should be used to communicate to employees. Possible methods include:

- individual briefings;
- team briefings;
- road shows and open days;

FIGURE 12.9 Example of total reward statement

Total reward statement		
Pay	Basic annual salary	£30,000
	Bonus	£3,000
	Total	£33,000
Employee benefits	Retirement, life insurance and ill health	£5,000
	Holidays	£1,000
	Other fringe benefits (subsidized meals, employee assistance programme, concierge service, voluntary benefits, staff discount, free car parking)	£2,000
	Total	£8,000
Total remuneration		£41,000
Other rewards/ benefits	Learning and development programmes Further education assistance Flexible hours Additional maternity/paternity leave	

- intranet and internet, including bulletin boards;
- CDs;
- newsletters;
- individual letters to employee's home address;
- meetings, Q&A sessions, focus groups;
- demonstrations with computer modelling;
- telephone and e-mail helplines;
- one-to-one consultations.

Tool 13
Pay reviews

Introduction

Pay reviews are general or 'across-the-board' reviews in response to movements in the cost of living or market rates, or following pay negotiations with trade unions, or individual reviews that determine the pay progression of individuals in relation to their performance or contribution. They are one of the most visible aspects of reward management (the other is job grading) and are an important means of implementing the organization's reward policies and demonstrating to employees how these policies operate.

Even where pay increases include a performance element, employees typically expect that pay reviews will maintain the purchasing power of their pay by compensating for increases in the cost of living. They will want their levels of pay to be competitive with what they could earn outside. And they will want to be rewarded fairly and equitably for the contribution they make.

Purpose and contents of the tool

The purpose of the tool is to describe how to conduct general and individual pay reviews. It is set out under the following headings:

- Review policy;
- Conducting general reviews;
- Conducting individual reviews.

Pay review policy

An organization's overall pay policy should include what will be taken into account in conducting pay reviews. Where this has not been clearly laid out it is necessary to agree the factors that will be taken into account in conducting reviews, so that the pay review process can be clearly explained

FIGURE 13.1 Checklist: pay review policy

Factor	Issues
Cost of living	Which index or indices to use: retail prices index (with or without mortgage interest rates) or consumer prices index, or reference to all of them?
Pay settlements	How sector specific does this need to be? What regular sources of information can you identify that will enable you to take a consistent view of rates of increase each year?
Individual performance	Is there an agreed process for doing this?
Marketability	To what extent will the organization take into account market movement for specific jobs or groups (families) of jobs?
Internal relativities	Do you need to have scope in your review to adjust for any anomalies that might have arisen between staff, eg due to recruitment salaries?
Affordability	Has the review policy included reference to affordability?

to all employees and any managers that may be involved in making pay recommendations. These factors are summarized in Figure 13.1.

General reviews

General or across-the-board reviews take place when all employees are given an increase in response to any combination of general market rate movements, increases in the cost of living, or union negotiations. General reviews may be combined with individual reviews. Alternatively the general review may be conducted separately to enable better cost control and to focus employees' attention on the performance-related aspect of their remuneration.

Some organizations have completely abandoned the use of across-the-board reviews. They argue that the decision on what people should be paid should be an individual matter, taking into account the personal contribution people are making and their 'market worth' – how they as individuals are valued in the marketplace. This enables the organization to adopt a more flexible approach to allocating pay increases in accordance with the perceived value of individuals to the organization.

The steps required to conduct a general pay review are:

1 Obtain initial budgetary guidelines.
2 Analyse data on pay settlements made by comparable organizations and rates of inflation.

3 Calculate costs.

4 Get budget approval – including parameters for negotiations, if appropriate.

5 Conduct negotiations with trade unions as required, liaising as appropriate with senior management on budgetary constraints.

6 Adjust the pay structure – by either increasing the pay brackets of each grade by the percentage general increase or by increasing pay reference points by the overall percentage and applying different increases to the upper or lower limits of the bracket, thus altering the shape of the structure.

7 Inform employees.

Individual reviews

Individual pay reviews determine contingent pay increases or bonuses. Individual awards may be based on ratings, an overall assessment that does not depend on ratings or ranking as discussed below.

Individual pay reviews based on ratings

Managers propose increases on the basis of their performance ratings within a given pay review budget and in accordance with pay review guidelines. Of the respondents to the e-reward 2009 survey of contingent pay, 80 per cent used ratings to inform contingent pay decisions.

There is a choice of methods. The simplest way is to have a direct link between the rating and the pay increase, as in Figure 13.2.

FIGURE 13.2   Example of link between rating and pay increase

Rating	% increase
A	6
B	4
C	3
D	2
E	0–1

This approach was used by 36 per cent of the respondents to the e-reward 2009 survey.

A more sophisticated approach is to use a pay matrix as illustrated in Figure 13.3. This indicates the percentage increase payable for different

FIGURE 13.3   A pay matrix

	Percentage pay increase according to performance rating and position in pay range (compa-ratio)			
Rating	Position in pay range			
	80%–90%	91%–100%	101%–110%	111%–120%
Excellent	12%	10%	8%	6%
Very effective	10%	8%	6%	4%
Effective	6%	4%	3%	0
Developing	4%	3%	0	0
Ineligible	0	0	0	0

performance ratings according to the position of the individual's pay in the pay range. This is sometimes referred to as an individual 'compa-ratio' and expresses pay as a percentage of the mid point in a range. A compa-ratio of 100 per cent means that the salary would be at the mid point. This approach usually assumes that the effective performer who is at or close to mid point will receive an increase that keeps their pay market-competitive.

This approach was used by 41 per cent of the respondents to the e-reward 2009 survey.

Linking pay reviews to performance reviews

Many people argue that linking performance management too explicitly to pay prejudices the essential developmental nature of performance management. However, realistically it is accepted that decisions on performance-related or contribution-related increases have to be based on some form of assessment. One solution is to 'decouple' performance management and the pay review by holding them several months apart, and 47 per cent of the respondents to the e-reward 2009 survey did this. There is still a read-across but it is not so immediate. Some try to do without formulaic approaches (ratings and pay matrices) altogether, although it is impossible to dissociate contingent pay completely from some form of assessment.

Doing without ratings

Of the respondents to the 2009 e-reward survey of contingent pay, 20 per cent did without ratings. One respondent explained that in the absence of ratings, the approach they used was 'informed subjectivity', which meant considering ongoing performance in the form of a broad overview of overall contribution.

Some companies require managers to take a range of factors into account in making pay recommendations. Managers propose where people should be placed in the pay range for their grade, taking into account their contribution and pay relative to others in similar jobs, their potential, the relationship of their current pay to market rates. The decision may be expressed in the form of a statement that an individual is now worth £30,000 rather than £28,000. The increase is 7 per cent, but what counts is the overall view about the value of a person to the organization, not the percentage increase to that person's pay.

Ranking

Ranking is carried out by managers who place staff in a rank order according to an overall assessment of relative contribution or merit, and then distribute performance ratings through the rank order. The top 10 per cent could get an A rating, the next 15 per cent a B rating and so on. The ratings determine the size of the reward. A forced ranking or 'vitality curve' system may be used to compel managers to conform to predetermined proportions of staff in each grade. But ranking depends on fair, consistent and equitable assessments, which cannot be guaranteed, and assumes that there is some sort of standard distribution of ability across the organization, which may not be the case.

Guidelines to managers on conducting individual pay reviews

Whichever approach is adopted, guidelines have to be issued to managers on how they should conduct reviews. These guidelines should stipulate budgetary constraints and may indicate the maximum and minimum increases that can be awarded, with a indication of how awards could be distributed, eg when the budget is 4 per cent overall, it might be suggested that a 3 per cent increase should be given to the majority of their staff and the others given higher or lower increases as long as the total percentage increase does not exceed the budget. Managers in some companies are instructed that they must follow a forced pattern of distribution (a forced-choice system) but only 8 per cent of the respondents to the 2003 CIPD survey (Armstrong and Baron, 2004) used this method.

To help them to explore alternatives, managers may be provided with a spreadsheet facility in which the spreadsheets contain details of the existing rates of staff and recent pay review history, which can be used to model alternative distributions on a 'what if' basis. Managers may also be encouraged to fine-tune their pay recommendations to ensure that individuals are on the right track within their grade according to their level of performance, competence and time in the job compared with their peers. To do this, managers need guidelines on typical rates of progression in relation to performance, skill or competence, and specific guidance on what they can and should do. They also need information on the relative positions of their staff in the pay structure in relation to the policy guidelines.

The final stage in the review process should include a formal review of pay proposals for the purpose of ensuring consistency of approach across the organization by relevant groupings, such as grade, department and gender plus any other equality monitoring criteria used by the organization. This review can also be used to ensure that the proposals are affordable.

Steps required to conduct an individual pay review

1 Agree budget.
2 Prepare and issue guidelines on the size, range and distribution of awards and on methods of conducting the review.
3 Ensure that managers have completed individual performance reviews.
4 Provide advice and support.
5 Review proposals against budget and guidelines; moderate proposals across different parts of the organization if necessary to ensure consistency of approach and agree modifications to proposals if required.
6 Summarize and cost proposals and obtain approval.
7 Update payroll.
8 Inform employees.

References

Armstrong, M and Baron, A (2004) *Performance Management: Action and Impact*, CIPD, London
Survey of Contingent Pay (2009) e-reward, Stockport

Tool 14
Evaluating reward

Introduction

Reward evaluation is the process of assessing the effectiveness of existing or new reward policies and practices. In essence, it is the comparison of reward outcomes with objectives to answer the question of how far the reward system has achieved its purpose and to indicate what actions are required.

The process of reward evaluation

The process of reward evaluation is illustrated in Figure 14.1.

Purpose and contents of the tool

The CIPD 2009 reward management survey established that only 32 per cent of respondents assessed the impact of their reward practices. In view of the amount of money and time invested in reward management, the degree of effort devoted to reward innovation and the importance attached to getting reward management right, this is a remarkably low proportion. The purpose of this tool is to provide guidance on how to remedy this shortfall by formal evaluation processes.

The tool is set out under the following headings:

- Aims;
- Fundamental questions;
- Methods of evaluation;
- Use of measurements, including the outcome of engagement surveys;
- Reaching a conclusion.

FIGURE 14.1   The process of reward evaluation

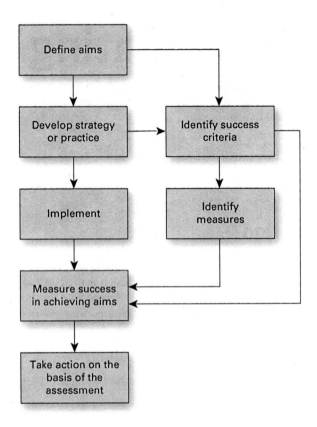

Aims

It is necessary to be clear about the aims of reward evaluation before planning to undertake it. Typical aims are:

- to find out how well established reward policies and practices are working and identify any problems;
- to establish whether reward innovations are functioning as planned and achieving the objectives set for them;
- to ensure that value for money is obtained from the different parts of the reward system;
- to provide the evidence required to indicate what needs to be done to improve reward effectiveness.

FIGURE 14.2   Checklist: fundamental questions on reward effectiveness

- Does the reward system meet the needs of the organization and its stakeholders?
- To what extent does the system achieve its goals?
- How well have the reward changes been implemented, and to what extent are they delivering on the reward goals and principles set out?
- Have there been any serious problems and if so have they been dealt with?
- Given what has been learnt, will any changes in design and or process improve the effectiveness of the reward system?
- How are we going to review and assess their effectiveness on an ongoing basis, and perhaps in some detail after a sufficient time has elapsed to witness the full impact of any changes?
- How are the organizational and external environment and context for the reward schemes changing? How might we therefore need to modify our schemes and processes to continue progressing towards our defined goals and continuing to improve effectiveness?

Fundamental questions

The checklist set out in Figure 14.2 contains a number of fundamental questions that need to be answered when considering reward evaluation.

Methods of evaluation

The main methods of evaluation are:

- against goals and success criteria;
- against external benchmarks;
- a four level evaluation framework;
- return on investment calculations.

These can be used singly or in combination.

Evaluation of existing practices against goals and success criteria

A success criterion indicates the conditions that exist when a reward objective has been achieved or a reward practice has worked well. A good success criterion should:

- be derived from a clear statement of objectives;
- illuminate the conditions that exist when the objective has been achieved;

FIGURE 14.3   Possible evaluation criteria for assessing reward effectiveness

Reward goals	Evaluation criteria
Reinforces and convergent with the business strategy and supports organization values, eg supports customer service, quality, etc.	Key business goals evident in incentive plans, performance assessment criteria, etc. Financial and non-financial recognition for behaviours in line with strategy and values. Clear reward strategy and annual plan in support of business strategy and plans. Overall staff productivity and return on staff costs versus competition – profit or sales per employee, value added, etc.
Rewards performance and contribution	Appropriate forms of rewarding performance and contribution in place – individual/team, short/long term, etc. Proportion of staff covered by methods of rewarding performance and contribution. Rewards effectively integrated with performance management process. Risk assessment of bonus plan design – fixed/variable mix, range of performance measures, etc. Clear demonstration of return on costs of bonus and incentive plans. Employee opinions that performance is rewarded and managed effectively.
Externally competitive, to recruit and retain	Use of external surveys and labour market analysis. Actual market position compared to desired. Ratio of job offers/acceptances. Staff involuntary turnover/resignation rates and retention of high performance/key skill staff. Employee opinions that rewards are competitive.
Develops employee engagement	Surveyed engagement levels, as well as satisfaction with pay and rewards. Staff turnover and absence levels. Productivity/added value compared with competitors.
Customized to meet needs of different employees	Flexible reward arrangements provided. Take-up and level of activity in flexible rewards. Justified variations between reward practices in different parts of the organization. Managers feel reward arrangements are flexible and meet their needs.
Cost effective and affordable	Variance in pay and reward costs with business performance.
Fair and legally compliant	Equal pay reviews carried out and acted upon. Reward and HR processes in place to ensure fair treatment, eg job evaluation, appeals, etc. Employee opinions on fair pay and treatment, overall and by key demographic groups.
Controlled and efficient to administer	Administration costs compared with competitors. Actual service levels versus plan. Number of breaches of policy/procedure.
Flexible, able to change	Evidence of reward changes being successfully introduced on a regular basis. Reward reviews undertaken on an annual/regular basis. Evidence of addressing tough situations, eg pensions deficits.

- enable the measures that can be used to establish success to be identified; ideally these should be quantifiable, but qualitative measures may have to be adopted as long as they indicate clearly what success means;
- facilitate the evaluation of effectiveness.

Examples of the criteria that can be used for evaluation by comparison with reward goals and success criteria are shown in Figures 14.3 and 14.4.

Evaluation against external benchmarks

External surveys of good practice in comparable organizations can reveal gaps in the provisions for reward and areas where improvements or changes can usefully be made.

A four-level evaluation framework

The following four-level evaluation framework follows the well established pattern established by Kirkpatrick (1983) for measuring training effectiveness. Like Kirkpatrick's system, it can be used to evaluate the overall impact of reward practices, or it can focus on specific aspects of reward.

- Level 1: immediate reaction to reward management policies and practices, including the fair, equitable and efficient administration of pay and benefit systems and the provision of competitive rates of pay.
- Level 2: evidence of improvements in individual performance, engagement and positive discretionary effort as a result of reward initiatives and practices.
- Level 3: evidence of the impact of reward initiatives and practices on overall levels of engagement, attraction and retention rates and absenteeism, or on the performance of specific activities or functions such as customer service, sales, operations and distribution.
- Level 4: evidence of the impact of reward initiatives and practices on the overall performance of the organization in such terms as financial and business outcomes, productivity and the achievement of competitive advantage.

Return on investment as a method of evaluation

The pressure to produce financial justifications for any organizational activity has increased the interest in using return on investment (ROI) as a criterion for assessing the overall impact of reward innovations on organizational performance. It is calculated as:

$$\frac{Benefits\ (\text{£}) - costs\ (\text{£})}{Costs\ (\text{£})} \times 100$$

FIGURE 14.4 Reward innovation and change objectives and success criteria

Reward innovation and change objective	Success criteria: This objective will have been successfully achieved when:
Develop performance culture	Reports of performance reviews show that performance has improved. There is evidence of improvement from other performance indicators.
Enhance engagement	Scores in the engagement survey have increased by x%.
Increase overall employee satisfaction with rewards	Scores in the rewards survey have increased by x%.
Increase key staff retention levels	Employee turnover for key categories of staff has reduced by x%.
Attract high-quality applicants	Surveys of new starters reveal that x% of them were attracted by the employee value proposition offered by the firm.
Develop employee value proposition	There is evidence that attraction and retention rates have improved.
Enhance pay competitiveness	Survey data shows that pay levels are competitive in line with market stance policy.
Increase employee satisfaction with contingent pay decisions	Scores in the contingent pay section of the rewards survey have increased by x%.
Replace decayed job evaluation scheme and use to develop new grade structure	The evaluation scheme is accepted as fair by staff. The cost of administering the scheme is within budget. Successful appeals against gradings are less than x% of staff. The cost of implantation does not exceed x% of payroll.
Introduce career family structure to support career planning	There is evidence that career ladders defined as competency levels are being used to guide career planning and development.
Reduce grade drift	There is evidence that regradings are being properly justified by job evaluation.
Introduce contribution-related pay scheme	There is evidence that it has improved performance. Staff feel that the scheme fairly recognizes their contribution.
Conduct an equal pay review and act on it	Equal pay review conducted as planned. Action taken which reduces the pay gap by x%.
Introduce flexible benefits	Take-up of scheme. Level of satisfaction in reward attitude survey.

Reward measurement

The purpose of measuring rewards is to analyse and interpret data collected by a formal or informal reward review as a basis for evaluating the effectiveness of reward policy and practice and for informing reward development decisions. The process of measurement involves:

- setting reward goals and success criteria, linked to the business and HR strategy and vision, and deciding what improvement is wanted and where it is essential; also deciding whether reward measurement needs to be part of a wider human capital management exercise;
- specifying and gathering the relevant information, or putting processes in place to gather it;
- analysing, monitoring and drawing conclusions from that information;
- taking action and making changes to improve effectiveness, which may well be improvements to the effectiveness measures as well as the reward practices themselves;
- analysing the results of employee opinion surveys, especially engagement surveys.

The principles for using measures are:

- Measure the right things – measure activities that directly contribute to an organization's performance.
- Clearly communicate what will be measured – measures that are ill defined and/or not communicated will not be used or understood.
- Consistently apply the measures – measures should be applied consistently to all units of the organization; failure to do so will result in loss of support for the system.
- Act on the measures – the measurement data must be used in a constructive way. Not using the data or misapplying the data will have the same results – a lack of support for the measurement system.

A list of commonly used measures under different assessment headings is set out in Figure 14.5.

FIGURE 14.5   Commonly used reward measures

Assessment area	Measures
Productivity, performance and reward costs	Productivity per employee
	Profit, value added or sales per employee
	Trends in performance appraisal ratings
	Total pay and reward costs compared to competition
Financial rewards	Return on investments in contingent pay
	Surveyed contingent pay scheme satisfaction rates
Employment	Employee turnover rates
	Employee absence rates
	Retention (survival rates) of high-performance/key-skill staff
	Ratio of job offers/acceptances
	Time taken to fill vacancies
	Proportion of vacancies filled by people who fully meet the specification
Reward management general	Actual market position compared with policy market stance
	Take-up and level of activity in flexible rewards.
	Reduction in gender pay gap following equal pay reviews
Engagement and satisfaction with rewards	Trends in surveyed overall employee engagement levels through engagement surveys
	Trends in surveyed employee satisfaction with rewards
	Employee opinions that rewards are competitive
	Employee opinions that performance is rewarded and managed effectively
	Manager opinions that reward arrangements meet their needs

Engagement survey

The achievement of higher levels of engagement is an important aim of reward management. It is therefore necessary to measure levels of engagement, establish trends in those levels, identify the reasons for those trends and, as far as possible, establish how those trends have been influenced by reward practices, especially innovations. An example is given in Figure 14.6.

FIGURE 14.6 Example of engagement survey

	Engagement survey Please place a tick in the box that most closely fits your opinion					
	Opinion	**Strongly agree**	**Inclined to agree**	**Neither agree nor disagree**	**Inclined to disagree**	**Strongly disagree**
1	I am very satisfied with the work I do.					
2	My job is interesting.					
3	I know exactly what I am expected to do.					
4	I am prepared to put myself out to do my work.					
5	My job is not very challenging.					
6	I am given plenty of freedom to decide how to do my work.					
7	I get plenty of opportunities to learn in this job.					
8	The facilities/equipment/tools provided are excellent.					
9	I do not get adequate support from my boss.					
10	My contribution is fully recognized.					
11	The experience I am getting now will be a great help in advancing my future career.					
12	I find it difficult to keep up with the demands of my job.					
13	I have no problems in achieving a balance between my work and my private life.					
14	I like working for my boss.					
15	I get on well with my work colleagues.					
16	I think this organization is a great place in which to work.					
17	I believe I have a good future in this organization.					
18	I intend to go on working for this organization.					
19	I am not happy about the values of this organization – the ways in which it conducts its business.					
20	The products/services provided by this organization are excellent.					

Reaching a conclusion

As described above, there is a wealth of evaluation methods and ways of measuring effectiveness. The starting point is to have a realistic view of what needs to be achieved and what is achievable. It is next a matter of answering the question posed by Corby *et al* (2003): 'Does it work?' This means, of course, deciding in advance what working effectively looks like and then collecting whatever information is available to provide evidence on what is happening and guidance on anything that needs to be done. Corby and colleagues advise sensibly that it is necessary to focus on evaluation in only a few key areas rather than compiling a wish list, use existing mechanisms such as employee attitude surveys and human capital reports as far as possible and consider perceptions and qualitative criteria, not just 'hard' cost and business figures.

References

Corby, S *et al* (2003) *Does it work? Evaluating a new pay system*, University of Greenwich, London

Reward Management 2009: A Survey of Policy and Practice (2009) CIPD, London